The Life of Saint Peter

Immortals of Philosophy and Religion

The Life of
SAINT PETER

by W. Norman Pittenger
S. T. D.

FRANKLIN WATTS, INC.
845 Third Avenue / New York, N. Y. 10022

Other *Immortals* by the author:

Henry VIII of England
The Life of Jesus Christ
The Life of Saint Paul
Martin Luther
Richard the Lion-hearted
Saint Thomas Aquinas

SBN 531-00963-7
Copyright © 1971 by Franklin Watts, Inc.
Library of Congress Catalog Card Number: 70-134659
Printed in the United States of America

ACKNOWLEDGEMENT
Material appearing on pages 42, 59, 87, 93-94, from
Peter: Disciple, Apostle, Martyr, by Oscar Cullmann,
translated by Floyd V. Filson. Second Revised Edition.
© scm Press, Ltd., 1962. Published in the U.S.A. 1962,
by The Westminster Press. Used by permission.

Contents

Preface

In a book about the development and meaning of the books in the New Testament part of the Bible, Principal T.A.G. Baker of Wells College, in England, speaks about Saint Peter in these words: "We know all that we need to know about Peter—the warmly human saint, the first witness to the resurrection [of Christ], the chief of the apostles, the rock on which the Church of Christ was built." Baker goes on to remark that the two letters in the New Testament which are attributed to Peter are likely to be what scholars call pseudonymous—that is, they are not by Peter himself but by some other, later Christian who thought to honor the saint by making him the author.

Whatever we may think about this view of the so-called Petrine letters, Principal Baker has admirably summed up why we should be interested in Peter himself. He has stated in a few phrases why Peter must be regarded as an immortal of religious history. As Baker says, here was a man who was, first of all, a "warmly human saint"—one who appeals to us because he was a typical man, with enthusiasms and defects. Here was a man who is portrayed in the stories in the New Testament, which we call the gospels, as "the first witness to the resurrection" of Jesus Christ. Here was one who became, very soon after that resurrection, "the chief of the apostles," whom even Saint Paul—who in many ways disagreed with Peter—honored and respected as the head of the company of Christian leaders. And perhaps most important of all, here was the one who was "the rock on which the Church of Christ was built."

That last assertion is demonstrated in many ways, not least because the head of the largest body of Christians in the world—the pope, or bishop of Rome—is called "the successor of Peter," occupying "the Fisherman's throne," and regarded by millions of Christians as continuing the same function which Saint Peter performed. Non-Roman Catholics, too, acknowledge Peter as "the rock." How could they do otherwise, when the Jesus whom they venerate spoke of Peter as precisely "the Rock on which I shall build my church"?

Thus, there is good reason to know as much as we

can about Saint Peter. But problems abound when we try to get this knowledge, since the available material includes fairly undisputed factual data, much uncertain tradition, collections of legends, and the like. The purpose of this book is to sort out this material, to try to get at the man Peter and his experiences, to present the faith that animated him, to tell how the stories grew up about him, and, finally, to speak of his place both in Rome, the "Eternal City," and also in the Christian Church which was built upon him as "the rock."

I am indebted to many books and to many scholars for help in preparing this study. Above all, I owe much to Dr. Oscar Cullmann's great work, *Peter: Disciple, Apostle, Martyr.* I refer to it those who wish to read the most competent scholarly volume recently written on the subject. To the others who have helped me I extend my thanks, especially to my colleagues on the Faculty of Divinity at the University of Cambridge. For all that I have written, of course, I must assume responsibility.

W. NORMAN PITTENGER

Note: In referring to incidents in the gospels and elsewhere in the New Testament, I have not resorted to the device appropriate in a scholarly book—namely, the continual noting of specific verse and chapter references. To have done so would have impeded the flow of the narrative and turned what is intended as a straightforward biographical and appreciative sketch into an academic exercise. The reader who wishes to check references will find a useful source in the article on Peter in the *Interpreter's Bible Dictionary* (see the bibliography) .

Quotations from the Bible are either from the Revised Standard Version or, more frequently, the writer's own translation of the Greek text.

The Life of Saint Peter

1

Why Read About Saint Peter?

Perhaps some of the readers of this book have traveled in Italy and have visited, in the city of Rome, the magnificent basilica of Saint Peter's. It is located across the Tiber River from the "downtown center" of Rome and is now approached by a new avenue leading into the great forecourt. The visitor must walk across the vast piazza and then up the long stairs that lead to the church itself. He enters the basilica by the great doors, crossing the wide narthex (vestibule), and, finally, passing through another set of doors into the enormous building. The length and width and spaciousness of the church are almost overwhelmingly impressive. At the chapel on the right, near the entrance, is Michelangelo's beautiful and moving *Pietà* —a representation of Saint Mary holding in her arms the body of her dead son Jesus, after he was taken down from the cross.

As the visitor strolls down the long nave toward the crossing, he will see three things. First, he will note the Latin words carved in gold, high up on the far wall. Their translation is, "Thou art Peter, and upon this rock I will build my church." Then he will see, in the crossing itself, what seems like a shrine, with stairs leading down to an underground chapel. This is the traditional approach to the place where Peter was buried, and a crowd of pilgrims will probably be kneeling around the opening. Finally, on the right side of the nave, just before the crossing, the visitor will see a statue. It shows Peter seated on a chair or throne. One foot is thrust out, and a toe of that foot is polished smooth by the millions of times it has been kissed by worshiping men, women, and children, who, in this way, acknowledged their reverence for the man whom the statue represents.

Those three things, viewed by everyone who enters the greatest church building in Christendom, as it has been called, help us to see why we should read about Saint Peter. First, whatever may be our religious convictions, or even if we have no convictions at all, the fact must be recognized that the Roman Catholic Church, with its millions of adherents throughout the world, acknowledges Peter as the rock upon which the Church is founded. And, indeed, all Christians—Protestant, Eastern Orthodox, Roman Catholic—who read the New Testament know that in the first of the gospels Jesus says to Peter exactly the words engraved on the basilica wall: "Thou art Peter, and upon this rock I will build my church."

Second, the opening down to the crypt is the way to the place where by tradition—and almost certainly in fact—Peter was buried after being martyred by the Roman authorities under the emperor Nero. He was martyred simply because he *was* a Christian. Ancient tradition says that Peter was killed in Rome. Tradition also tells us that Paul, the great missionary to the Gentiles, was also martyred in Rome—in this case, killed by a sword.

The year of both deaths was A.D. 64, more than nineteen hundred years ago. The two greatest leaders of the primitive Christian community both died in Rome, under the same emperor, and in the same persecution when a scapegoat was being sought for the terrible fire which rumor said that Nero himself started. The scapegoat was the Christian congregation in the city, a group dangerous to the welfare of the state. It is said that Peter and Paul were there at the time. They were among those—perhaps chief among them—who were sought out and killed.

Third, the statue of Saint Peter tells of the veneration felt for the martyred man. In some fashion, Peter has caught the imagination of Christians. Perhaps it is because he is acknowledged as "the rock." Perhaps it is because each succeeding head of the Roman Catholic Church is called "the successor of Peter." Whatever the reason, the veneration is great.

Yet, there is still another reason for interest in Peter. It is simply that he figures very largely in the New Testament itself. He appears again and again in the accounts of the life of Jesus. Peter is the one who, in the Acts of the Apostles, preaches the first Christian sermon, on the Day of Pentecost. He is the one whom Paul sought out to learn about the story of Jesus. It is to Peter that we owe the understanding, which he himself learned from experience, that "to God nothing is common" and that God wills that all men, whether Jew or non-Jew, "should be saved." And in the New Testament there are two documents which are attributed to Peter, one a long essay dealing with the life of the baptized Christian, the other a shorter letter about faithfulness in times of disaster and danger.

In these and other ways, Peter is an inescapable figure in the account of the very first days of the Christian Church. Whatever we can learn about him will help us in understanding the Christian faith itself. And that understanding is essential if we are to have any comprehension of the history of Europe—and eventually of the rest of the world—in the years since the birth of Jesus Christ.

There can be no doubt that Paul is the great theologian, as well as the great missionary leader, of the earliest Christian community of believers. Certainly we know a good deal about him and his thought, through his letters and because the Acts of the Apostles is so largely concerned with his travels. One unfortunate consequence, however, of this knowledge about Paul is that other Christians of that period tend to be forgotten or overlooked. The disciple called John, for example, is often not given due place when scholars write about the thought of early Christianity and about how Christian theology developed.

The same is true of Peter. He has been overshadowed by his fellow martyr in Rome. In a sense, that is just, since it was Paul who did most to bring Christianity to the non-Jewish world. But in another sense, it is unjust to the one whom Jesus made the human leader of his band of followers. And it is surely misleading, since the result has been a tendency for Christians to be almost solely Pauline (as a theologian would say) in their way of interpreting the Christian message.

But it is Peter who proclaims the Christian message in its simplest form. First, Jesus Christ is not simply a historical personage who lived long ago and is now dead. On the contrary, he is the living Lord who is still present with those who believe in him. Second, Jesus did not mysteriously appear; he came as a Jew who brought to fulfillment all that the Jews—and other people of all races—had expected and hoped for and believed. Third, those who will commit themselves to this Jesus will be brought into a new and intimate relationship with the God who "sent" Jesus into the world. They will be given a new life—a life so rich and full that it amounts to "salvation" or genuine "wholeness." Finally, the way to a new life is by "changing your mind," altering your attitude to life by accepting this Jesus, and then by participating in the rite that brings one into the Christian fellowship —the rite of baptism, or immersion in water.

So, long before the conversion of Paul, Peter had begun the work of bringing others into the Christian life. Of course, he was not acting alone; the other first Christians were with him, having shared his experience and doubtless also shared his proclamation. But the narrative represents Peter as the leader, the one who spoke on their behalf, the man who was the chief in the first proclamation of the Christian message or gospel.

In order to gain some understanding of Peter,

both as a man and as a leader of the first Christian Church, it is necessary to know something about the country and people to which he belonged.

Peter was a Jew. That meant that he lived in that small land at the eastern end of the Mediterranean Sea which we now know as Israel, or Palestine as it used to be called. During his lifetime—as well as decades before and a long time afterward—Palestine was a part of the great Roman Empire. Since Peter came from the northern area, known as Galilee, his home was in a part of the land that still retained a local ruler. However, the ruler was only a puppet for the imperial power. When the Romans had occupied the whole country, they had been willing to allow some independence to certain sections, under Roman supervision. In contrast, Jerusalem itself, as well as the countryside bordering it, was under the control of an appointed governor or procurator, a Roman official. The governor was Pontius Pilate, under whom Jesus was crucified about A.D. 27 or 28, and he had been sent from Rome to rule over what the Roman authorities regarded as a turbulent people.

Rome had not interfered with the religious beliefs and practices of the inhabitants, however. So long as the people behaved themselves, Rome was prepared to let them worship as they wished. Hence, the

7

Judaism which for so long had been identified with the lifeblood of the Jews continued without any interference.

In religious matters, the authority was the Great Sanhedrin, or council of the Jewish people, whose headquarters was in Jerusalem. The high priest, appointed annually with Roman approval, was the presiding official in the Sanhedrin. Even though Galilee was politically independent, in word at least, its religious life was centered in Jerusalem, the ancient capital city of the Jews.

Communication was not difficult between Galilee and Judah, where Jerusalem was situated. It was possible to go from one to the other by either of two routes. One was through Samaria, a small bit of land where the inhabitants were also Jews. However, because of certain beliefs and customs, the Samaritans were regarded by other Jews as being heretics. One New Testament reference says, "The Jews have no dealings with the Samaritans." For this reason, the second route was often chosen by travelers. It went somewhat to the east of Samaria, through a largely Romanized countryside.

Palestine is a hilly country, now arid and treeless for the most part. But in those early days it was much wooded and in some places highly cultivated. The Galilean area was remarkably fertile. There were farms and villages, and most of the inhabitants lived "on the land." Although there were no cities of any size, such towns as Nazareth, where Jesus lived, and Capernaum were important because of their locations on or near trade routes. Furthermore, since the Sea of Galilee, which forms the eastern boundary of that section, is a freshwater lake, there was much fishing, and a considerable number of the residents were engaged in this business.

Peter was a fisherman, as were others whom Jesus chose to be his disciples. On the whole, the fishermen were prosperous, since there was a great demand for their fish not only in Galilee itself but also in the adjacent country. Fish was a staple food for the Jews, who were forbidden to eat pork because of an ancient religious prohibition and who did not find it easy to secure other meats except lamb or mutton on festivals and great occasions.

To say that the Jewish religion was accepted by the people who lived in Palestine is perhaps putting it too mildly. It was, in fact, followed by many with extraordinary fervor, almost with fanaticism. This was because the ruling power was Gentile—that is, not Jewish—and the Jews were outraged at being controlled by people not of their own. Hence, they were likely to become vigorous and even bigoted in support of their inherited religion, which provided them with a sense of national identity and community. Yet, in the countryside and in the small towns, the details of the ancient Jewish Torah (the "Law" which was believed to have been given to the Jews from God through Moses) were far too complicated and detailed to permit complete obedience.

So, in reality, large numbers of people were, indeed, believers in, and followers of, the old Jewish customs, but with a certain laxity in actual practice. They were dismissed by the more zealous and fanatical as "people of the land," being regarded as lukewarm in their Judaism or at least uninstructed and easygoing about observing its requirements. Peter, like most of the others called by Jesus to be his close disciples, would have belonged to this less zealous group—as did Jesus himself.

The two principal groups of Jewish leaders were the Sadducees and the Pharisees. The former were representatives of the priestly families in Jerusalem, the richer and more established folk who cooperated with the Roman overlords and rejected the "newfangled" notions of the Pharisaic party.

The Pharisees were the most fanatical of all the Jewish people. They were strict followers of the ancient Torah and often had only contempt for the Gentiles who controlled their country. But in following the Law, the Pharisees used many interpretations.

This was because they saw that much in the Torah needed adaptation to the changing conditions in which people lived. So they built up what was styled "the tradition of the elders," a great mass of interpretive material that made it possible to relate the old requirements to contemporary situations. In doing this, however, they made matters even more complicated.

One example will demonstrate this. In doing what was called "fencing the Law"—that is, protecting what were thought to be its basic requirements, yet adapting them to present situations—the Pharisees would look at a command and then develop the way in which it should be obeyed. For instance, one command said that no work of any kind should be performed on the Sabbath. The Pharisees would ask: What does work mean? Is walking to the synagogue, the Jewish place of worship, to be considered work? Is it work to feed one's sheep on that day? Is it work to prepare the meals to be eaten? And so it went . . . question followed question, until at length there was a long series of permissions and prohibitions that made it difficult, if not impossible, for simple, hard-working farmers or fishermen to comprehend, much less follow, the requirements.

The Pharisees themselves were meticulous in following the requirements. They regarded those who did not as disloyal Jews. On the other hand, there can be no doubt that the Pharisees were very good people. Perhaps they were too good, since they lacked sympathy and understanding of ordinary mortals and the problems they faced. This, indeed, was Jesus' own condemnation of the whole Pharisaic approach to religion. Instead of freedom in the service of God, it tended to substitute careful obedience to a mass of requirements which, however desirable in themselves, made religion a burden and a worry rather than a deliverance. The Pharisaic view was not an inspiration so much as a "yoke too grievous to be borne," as Jesus said.

There were other types of Jewish opinion besides the Sadducean and the Pharisaic. Some Jews were even more fanatical than the Pharisees in their opposition to Roman rule. These people were called the Zealots. Some of them were so strongly against the alien government that they were even prepared to kill foreigners.

Another group was the Essenes. A good deal has been learned about these people through excavations near the Dead Sea and the discovery of the so-called Dead Sea Scrolls. These Jews often lived in small communities of the faithful, observing the Torah as they understood it. They looked toward the day when God would deliver his people Israel from the Romans and would establish them once again in their own land, with other nations paying them honor as God's "specially chosen people." There is little doubt, according to scholars who have studied the Dead Sea Scrolls, that some of the ideas of the Essenes influenced early Christian thought. However, it is felt that this influence was not very large and was confined mainly to ways of interpreting or presenting the Christian faith rather than to making any important modifications in the faith itself.

In the city of Jerusalem, and perhaps in a few other places, there were some Jews who were "hellenized"—that is, who had adopted a good deal of the Greek culture of the time. They wore Greek clothing; they visited the gymnasium, a place for physical exercise; and they even attempted to find ways of stating Jewish beliefs in Greek idiom.

Greek, in this sense, includes the life in the eastern end of the Mediterranean, not only in the land of Greece. Greek ways of thinking and living were very prevalent in the Roman Empire as a whole, but especially in Asia Minor and in those parts of the European continent near the ancient Greek cities.

Thousands, maybe millions, of Jews lived out of their own country. They made up what was known as the *Diaspora,* or dispersion. Most were engaged in trade or other business in foreign territories. These people were very likely to be the most influenced by Greek ideas.

But even in Palestine itself many Jews were influenced by Greek thought. They were looked upon by the Pharisees as traitors to the traditional religion, and from time to time they experienced difficulties in Palestine because of their willingness to modify their inherited faith and ethics.

One consequence of the Roman occupation of Palestine was serious economic deprivation. Besides the payment of the Temple tax, which was used to support the great religious center in Jerusalem and to pay the priests who conducted the worship, there was very heavy taxation to maintain the occupying forces. It was the Roman custom to make the inhabitants of conquered lands pay for the army maintained there. The result of this taxation, especially when added to local taxes for puppet rulers and their courts, was widespread poverty and need. The ordinary people—"the people of the land," in particular—were hard hit. Some experts have concluded that the situation was, in fact, almost desperate, and that from time to time the uprisings of Jews in villages, or on occasion in Jerusalem, are explained by this desperate condition in which so many found themselves.

Taxes were collected by a despised class of men

who, in the translations of the New Testament, are called publicans. In England today this word means men who own or operate places where alcoholic drinks may be purchased. At that time the word meant simply "tax collectors."

Publicans were Jews, of course, but they were Jews who were used by the authorities to extort money from the people. The method of tax collection was barbarous. There was no such thing as regular assessments. On the contrary, the collector got an idea of what somebody could be made to pay, and then he proceeded to apply pressure to get the money. Not only did he have to secure money for the actual taxes, but he also had to support himself by what he could force people to pay him. Hence, he was regarded as a scoundrel and extortioner, and, indeed, as an enemy. No wonder then that when Jesus spoke to, and made friends with, some of these publicans, he was thought to be doing something wicked and scandalous.

Yet the tax collectors were as much victims of the system as anybody else. They were engaging in work which was necessary, even if they were hardly kind in doing it. The contempt in which they were held, especially by the Pharisees, can be seen in the gospel reports of people classing the publicans, along with prostitutes, as the most evil folk in the land.

These were some of the main issues of life in Peter's time. What of his religion, both as a faith and a practice? What was Judaism like?

There were many varieties of Jewish belief and life, many different interpretations, and many schools of thought. But there was some genuine agreement about what constituted a faithful Jew. He was racially a member of the people whose homeland was Palestine, even if he happened to be living elsewhere. He attended the Sabbath services in the synagogue or local congregation, where each week he heard readings from the ancient Scriptures, the singing of psalms, benedictions or prayers, and an exposition of the Torah. If a male, he had been circumcised according to the requirements of the Law. He accepted that Law or Torah, however he might "interpret it," as binding upon him. And so far as his knowledge and his situation permitted, he sought to obey the Law's mandates in the everyday affairs of life.

As a Jew he was bound in fellowship with every other Jew, whom he was supposed to help wherever possible or necessary—all Jews were brothers and all understood their obligation to give mutual assistance. Although most Jews lived at a great distance from Jerusalem, it was an act of piety to be present, if possible, at the worship of the Temple in that city. At the great feasts, the city was thronged with visitors, who came often at great expense and real hardship to fulfill this duty. In any event, every loyal Jew made his contribution to the support of the Temple worship and priesthood and regarded it as a great privilege to be able to do so.

What did a Jew believe? What was his "creed"? There was no specific Jewish creed, save the *Shema*: "Thou shalt love the Lord thy God with all thy heart and mind and soul," with its corollary in loving one's fellow Jew as one loved oneself. But if there was no such thing as a Jewish creed, there were, instead, accepted convictions which the pious Jew firmly believed. These convictions were few and simple.

1. God, whom the Jews called *Yahweh* (we wrongly translate this as "Jehovah"), is the creator of the world. He is the one and only God, maker of heaven and earth and of everything that is. (The Jew was a passionate monotheist—believer in but *one* God.)

2. God has chosen Israel to be his own special people. He did this first through calling Abraham, then through Moses, and, finally, showed his care by guarding and guiding the Jews throughout their history.

3. God has a purpose for his chosen people. This purpose is that they shall speak for him and act for him in the world, serving as "a light to lighten the

Gentiles." Sometimes the Jews took this to be a great privilege of which they should be proud. But their teachers insisted that it was a call to God's service and to the service of other nations and races, since only when people worship Yahweh and do his will can they find the peace and happiness which all men desire.

4. God has prepared a future for his people Israel. This future, sometimes called "the kingdom of God" (God's sovereign rule over the world), will be established by God in due course. When it comes, the Jewish people will be recognized as those who have known and done God's will. Their city Jerusalem, the "holy city," will be the religious center for all people. Their sufferings through the centuries will be vindicated and they themselves will be rewarded.

5. In doing this, God will also vindicate his own rule of the world and will demonstrate both his power and his goodness. Thus, his kingdom will be manifest and all men will acknowledge him as their God.

6. Finally, in working out his purpose for his chosen people, God has given them, through Moses, the Torah or Law—he has revealed his will and has shown how men are to live in obedience to that will. The faithful Jew will accept the Law as God's gracious gift to his people, will observe its requirements, and will find himself blessed in doing so.

In general, that is what the Jew believed. In addition, he might also believe that God would send his Anointed One, his *Messiah* (we use the Greek correlative "Christ" to express this idea), to be the agent to bring in his kingdom and restore all things to his will. Many, but not all, Jews accepted this view. Its importance shows itself in the meaning of the earliest Christian faith in Jesus, the prophet of Nazareth, as "the Christ of God." This is the faith which Peter himself affirmed on one notable occasion during Jesus' days on earth, and to which he gave himself as a preacher, apostle, and martyr.

2

The Call from Jesus

A map of Palestine will show a dot on the shores of the Sea of Galilee, indicating a small town called Bethsaida. According to John's gospel, this was Peter's birthplace.

Bethsaida does not actually exist today, but biblical scholars have decided, from bits of evidence, on the probable location. It was on the eastern bank of the River Jordan, where the river empties into that part of the Sea of Galilee which is also called the Lake of Gennesaret. The interesting thing about the particular location is that it was included within a section of Palestine that had many Gentile surroundings. In fact, Bethsaida was in the neighborhood of the towns that Gentiles, in this case Romans, had built and whose inhabitants were largely non-Jews. Nonetheless, the name of the place ("fisherman's city") is Jewish, and there can be little doubt that the town was itself a Jewish community. Yet, there would certainly have been Gentile influences there.

Matthew's gospel says that Peter was the son of a man called Jonah. He is described as "Simon Bar-Jonah," which means "Simon, son of Jonah." Jonah is an Aramaic abbreviation for the name John or Jonathan. This would indicate that Peter (or Simon as he was first called) came of a Jewish family who spoke Aramaic, the common popular language of the time. The old classical Hebrew was used only in learned circles, in religious services, and for formal purposes. Ordinary people used a kind of related dialect.

One reason for stressing Peter's Jewish family origins in a largely Gentile countryside is that it helps us to understand later references in the gospels and in the Acts of the Apostles. For one thing, it explains why Peter's brother, Andrew, is given what is obviously a Greek and not a Hebrew name. Even the name Simon has Greek associations. It explains the story of Philip, Peter's friend from Bethsaida, who also became a disciple of Jesus'. In John's gospel it is said that Philip was the man to whom the Gentiles (called Greeks) turned when they wished to have an interview with the Master.

Despite his background and the fact that he probably spoke the common Greek of the ordinary people —a type of language called *koine,* or common tongue —Peter was not a highly educated man. Indeed, there is a reference in Acts that describes him as "uneducated." This would mean that by the standards even of that time, whether Gentile or Jewish, Peter was not a person who had been "schooled." Probably he had never received any education beyond attending the school associated with the village synagogue. In such a school he would only learn a bit about the Jewish Scriptures, which we know as the Old Testament, and perhaps some fairly primitive arithmetic. It is likely that from a very early age he had worked with his father in the fish business, with no opportunity for proper schooling.

Peter later moved to the town of Capernaum where he continued his fishing business. In Mark's gospel Capernaum is given as his home when he met and first became a friend of Jesus'. As a fisherman, Peter evidently had a flourishing trade. He was associated with two other men—the "sons of Zebedee," James and John, who are said in Luke's gospel to be his "partners."

At Capernaum Peter encountered the young prophet from Nazareth. They struck up an acquaintance, and it is said that Jesus was often with Simon Peter, going to his home, meeting his family, and even (according to a hint in Matthew's gospel) living with him and his family for a time. Both the accounts in the gospels and a reference in one of Paul's letters indicate that Peter was married. But we are told nothing about his wife in any trustworthy records. There are legendary tales that speak of her martyrdom.

According to a reference in John's gospel, it seems that before Peter became an intimate associate and follower of Jesus', he (like his brother Andrew and others) had been profoundly interested in the preaching of John the Baptizer, also called John the Baptist. Perhaps, Peter had even been part of the circle that followed John and accepted his message.

John the Baptizer was a strange figure who suddenly appeared in the hill country of Palestine, announcing that the kingdom of God was soon to appear and demanding that the Jews prepare themselves for its coming. He was an ascetic, who lived on "locusts and wild honey," who wore the ragged clothes of an itinerant preacher, and whose fiery manner and vigorous words made a great impact on those who heard him.

John was utterly convinced that the "end of the age" was at hand. This meant that God was to come to his people in judgment, to sift the wheat from the tares (the good from the bad), and to recompense men for what they had done or had failed to do. God would come as fire, burning up all that was evil, and no man would be able to "abide the day of his coming." What was necessary, then, was repentance. No amount of ceremonial obedience to the Law would save people from "the wrath which is to come." What mattered was whether their hearts were right with God, and whether they had been just, honorable, and decent in their treatment of others.

Those who accepted the truth of John's preaching were to baptize themselves "for the remission of their sins," as a sign of their true repentance. John himself did not baptize them; he simply led them into the water where they immersed themselves. When they came up from the water of baptism, they were once again established as true Jews—a status that could not be achieved by simply belonging to the Jewish people by birth. In other words, John was asking the Jews to undergo the same ceremony, with the same repentance, which was expected when a Gentile was converted to the Jewish faith.

Jesus of Nazareth, a young artisan from a town in the hilly country back of the Sea of Galilee, had himself been attracted by John's preaching. He had undergone the baptism which John demanded, and it might have been thought that he was only another of John's followers. But on the occasion of his baptism, something happened to Jesus, as related in the several gospel stories. It is said that a dove descended upon Jesus or that he saw a dove coming down upon him. The dove symbolized divine peace and approval.

With the descent of the dove, Jesus heard God saying to him: "Thou art my beloved Son." It gave Jesus a sense of vocation. He was convinced that it was a call to him, demanding that he should take up the task of preaching God's kingdom. To make sure that this was indeed the case, he went off for some time— "forty days and forty nights"—into the wild country nearby in order to think things through and come to a decision about his vocation.

When Jesus returned, he was clear in his own mind that he had indeed been called. Not long afterward, John the Baptizer was falsely arrested by the authorities of the puppet king and was put into prison. Within a short time he was beheaded. Then Jesus began to act on his vocation. He started to move about the countryside, proclaiming, "The kingdom of God is at hand. Repent and believe this good news."

Good news . . . this was the difference between John and Jesus. The coming of the kingdom, as John had announced it, was anything but good news. Actually, it was very bad news, for it meant judgment and punishment. The God whom John talked about was the terrible God of fire, whose "fan was in his hand," who would "thresh the harvest floor," who would cast out the evildoers.

Jesus, on the other hand, thought of God in terms of love. His picture of God was that of a father who cares for his children, who wishes to help them, who understands and sympathizes with their failures even if he does not approve of those failures, and who will come, not to punish, but to save. In the Old Testament writings there is much material that provides that kind of picture of God, just as there is material that shows John's picture. Jesus chose to select and emphasize the loving and caring side. Perhaps this is why the common people heard Jesus "gladly," while they had listened to John with what amounted to terror and fear.

Doubtless, Jesus and Peter had known each other before Jesus began his preaching. But the summons to Peter to be one of Jesus' own company evidently came with a compulsion that was inescapable. The impression made by Jesus, when he "called" his disciples, was overwhelming. In Mark's gospel, it is explained in these simple words:

"And passing along by the Sea of Galilee, He [Jesus] saw Simon and Andrew his brother casting a net into the sea, for they were fishermen. And Jesus said to them, Follow me and I will make you become fishers of men. And immediately they left their nets and followed him. And going on a little farther, he saw James the son of Zebedee and John his brother, who were in the boat mending their nets. And immediately he called them; and they left their father Zebedee in the boat with the hired servants, and followed him . . ."

Maybe there had been some preparation for this call. Perhaps there had been discussion of Jesus' projected mission. Certainly all of them were aware of John the Baptizer's message. Nonetheless, there is a starkness and an immediacy about the call, and about the response to it, which is both startling and striking. Simon Peter, his brother Andrew, and their two associates in the fishing business were captured by this remarkable young man, who, like them, was in his late twenties or perhaps early thirties. There was nothing they could do but say "Yes." From that day forward they were his men. And Simon Peter, the simple fisherman from Bethsaida, was their leader under Jesus.

There has been much said about "gentle Jesus meek and mild." But the truth is that Jesus was every inch a man, whatever else he may have been. He was a workman, a village artisan (the word "carpenter" does not precisely, nor correctly, translate the Greek word in the gospels—*tekton*—which means a skilled workman or craftsman). Because people have long thought of Jesus as meek and mild, they have also incorrectly estimated his immediate companions. These disciples were, for the most part, workmen, too. Perhaps John, "the beloved disciple," was of a more gentle disposition, but Peter and the rest were rough-and-ready countrymen, without much education in a formal sense and very definitely "men of the people."

The time that Jesus and the twelve disciples spent together was a hard life, involving physical effort, inadequate lodgings, and long treks through the country. Strength of body and character was needed, and exacting demands were also made upon the loyalty of the disciples. Jesus was not always easy to understand. Sometimes he seemed to speak almost in riddles. Thus, his followers needed strength of purpose and sharpness of mind. Once or twice Jesus said they were "dull in understanding." But certainly companionship with him sharpened their wits and gave them what today we would call spiritual insight.

From the day that Jesus called Peter, the new disciple was with his master. They spent all their time together, along with the others who had also been called. The twelve disciples constituted a closely knit group, although probably there were others who came and went. In this way, the twelve came to know, in a very real way, what Jesus was "up to" in his preaching and teaching, his healing and helping.

Finally, being with Jesus all the time, listening to him and working with him, Peter and the others experienced more than admiration and respect for their master. They began to love him, and within a short time to feel a certain reverence, even awe, in his presence. The gospel stories indicate that they felt compelled to speculate about who he could be—this man to whom they had committed themselves as disciples, who loved them as friends, yet presented them with incredibly difficult demands. In all these respects, Peter was typical of the others, but the gospel stories tell more about Peter than all the rest.

3

Peter in the Gospels

One way to gain an impression of the man that was
Simon Peter is to select a number of "moments"
in the gospel accounts where he is an important figure.
These records do not pretend to give a day-by-day
story, but are put together, in their present form, to
provide an impression of Jesus, especially as his followers understood him. So, too, they give an impression of those who were Jesus' companions.

The gospels are the first four books of the New
Testament, said to have been written by Mark (about
A.D. 65), Matthew (about A.D. 70 to 85), Luke (A.D.
80 to 90), and John (A.D. 95-105).

In all the gospels there is an account of what
might be described as Jesus' commissioning of his immediate disciples to act on his behalf "to preach and

to have authority to cast out demons." In Mark's, the commissioning is said to have taken place in "the hills," where Jesus went with his followers. There he appointed twelve of them, presumably symbolizing the twelve tribes of Israel, to "be with him" and to carry out, on his behalf, the same work that he himself was doing. After the commissioning, the disciples began to "go out, two by two," traveling through the country, healing the sick, and proclaiming the coming of the kingdom. Their work was crowned with success. They returned to tell Jesus how they had been able, "in his name," to do what he had sent them to do.

During the commissioning it is also said that Peter was given his name—"Simon whom he surnamed Peter." Why was his name changed? In the famous and much-disputed passage in Matthew's gospel (16:17ff.), Jesus says: "You are Rock, and upon this Rock I will build my Church . . ."

The point here is a pun. The word *cephas* in Hebrew is both a common noun for rock and a proper name for a man. In Greek, the word is *petra*, also a proper name and a common noun. So the statement is a half-joking, half-serious play on words by Jesus himself. He probably recognized in Peter a certain rocklike tenacity of purpose which was really his true character more than his impulsive, often impetuous, actions. Above all, Jesus would have seen the absolute firmness of Peter's dedication, his loyalty and utter devotion. Upon *this* it would be possible for Jesus to establish the kind of following—the Church—which was necessary if his message and work were to be continued.

Another gospel story tells of the "transfiguration" of Jesus. With Peter and the two brothers James and John, Jesus went to "a high mountain," where he engaged in prayer. It seems to have been a custom of Jesus to go, from time to time, to some lonely place where he would pray quietly.

The three disciples and Jesus were alone on the mountain, and as Jesus prayed, it seemed that he was "transfigured before them and his garments became glistening, intensely white, as no fuller [dyer] on earth could bleach them."

Exactly what occurred is not known. Most scholars today say that it was probably a vision on the part of the three friends, who came to understand something of the majesty and wonder of their master. Furthermore, it seemed that two Old Testament figures—Moses (representing the Law) and Elijah (representing the prophets)—were present with Jesus.

At this point, Simon Peter, in his great amazement and awe, cried out in these words: "Master, it is good for us to be here. Let us make three booths [coverings or places of abode], one for you, one for Moses, and one for Elijah." Peter's impetuosity is clearly demonstrated here. But before there could be any response, a voice spoke to them from "a cloud," saying, "This is my beloved Son. Listen to him."

Although the exact nature of the incident is not clear, the reference to the "cloud" is interesting. In Jewish thought a "cloud" (the *shekinah,* in Hebrew) was always associated with the presence and self-disclosure of God. Also, the words which were heard were a confirmation of what Jesus himself had heard after his own baptism. "Beloved Son" means in the Jewish idiom "he who has been chosen as Son." The command that the disciples were to "listen to him" signifies that the words which Jesus says are the very words which God wishes to be spoken to the world.

For our purpose, the important thing is that it was Peter who spoke. Once again he is the head of the band of disciples, and on their behalf he utters the comment which they would all have wished to make. The cloud passed, there was silence after the voice had spoken, and "suddenly, looking around, they no longer saw anyone with them save Jesus only." This remarkable experience gave Peter and the sons of Zebedee an even deeper awareness of the meaning of the master whom they served.

On several other occasions, the gospels tell of

Peter's questions to Jesus. For example, one story concerns the problem of forgiveness. Jesus had urged that only in forgiving one another can men live in peace and understanding.

Peter asks: "How many times shall I forgive my brother who sins against me?"

Jesus replies: "Until seventy times seven"—which means, again in Jewish idiom, *every time* that one's brother sins.

In another incident, after Jesus has told a parable, it is Peter who asks: "Do you speak this parable to us or to everybody?"

And again, when there is a discussion about the sort of reward that Jesus' followers may expect, Peter comments: "We have left everything and followed you."

Jesus replies with the promise that those who have done this will receive a reward, indeed, but not the sort of reward that worldly people would expect. Their reward is to be a share in the life of God's kingdom.

What appears over and over again is the fact that Peter is, as Matthew's gospel says, "the first" among the disciples. All these incidents, sayings, and reports indicate that when the events of Jesus' own life were recalled by others, the second name that was mentioned was that of Simon Peter. This establishes the basis for what later Christians began to call "the primacy of Peter." It is not a specially Roman Catholic idea, but simply a fact in the gospel traditions.

The most important of all the reported incidents is the confession made by Peter at Caesarea Philippi. This is the central moment in the life of Jesus, apart from his crucifixion and resurrection, since it establishes plainly his significance and the nature of his vocation. Our own interest, however, is in the part which Peter plays in the story. 1605009

Jesus is portrayed with his disciples on the way to the town of Caesarea Philippi, in the Gentile part of Palestine. He asks his disciples a very searching question: "Who do men say that I am?" The time had come to make clear the general opinion of him and his work.

The disciples tell him that some people think that he is John the Baptizer, come back to life after his execution. Others say that he is a reappearance of the Old Testament prophet Elijah. Still others say that he is at least one of the prophets returned to Israel.

Then Jesus asks: "But who do *you* say that I am?" He wants to know what his own immediate followers think about him.

Peter, in his impetuous way, blurts out the answer: "You are the Messiah."

In so doing, Peter declares that Jesus is no prophet who proclaims the coming of the kingdom. Rather, Jesus is God's own representative who will bring in that kingdom. Here is faith, indeed. Peter, the Rock, has said in so many words that Jesus is God's very own agent, given a divine commission and endowed with divine authority. Peter's faith in Jesus has enabled him to see more deeply than others just who this master really is.

In Matthew's account of the incident, Jesus then remarks that Peter's insight is not of "flesh and blood"; it is no merely human evaluation. It is much more profound than that. "My father who is in heaven has revealed this to you"—which is to say, it is by divine inspiration that Simon Peter has been enabled to discern who Jesus really and truly is and what his vocation means.

Then Jesus begins to tell his disciples that they must not speak about what Peter has said. He teaches them that the Son of Man must suffer many things, and be rejected by the elders and the chief priests and the scribes, and be killed. Only when he has undergone these things will he be vindicated: "After three days he will rise from among the dead."

But this foretelling of suffering and death is too much for Peter. How can the master whom he loves and in whom he has just declared his unswerving

faith be forced to undergo such things? So again he
cries: "God forbid, Master! This shall never happen to
you!"

Then comes the only word of rebuke which Jesus
is recorded to have given his chief disciple. "Get behind me, Satan!" Jesus says. "You are a stumbling
block, for you are not on God's side but on men's."

Why does Jesus speak in this apparently harsh
manner? Peter's own devotion, which will not let him
think of Jesus as undergoing anguish and eventual
death, is a denial of what Jesus himself believes to be
God's purpose for him. Such a denial can only be the
work of the powers that oppose God and God's will.
But the rebuke, sharp as it is, does not mean that
Peter loses his place in the company of disciples. On
the contrary, he remains as before. But because of
what Jesus has said, Peter is enabled to see even more
deeply into what his master's mission is all about.

Later on, when Jesus has overcome death by the
resurrection, it is to Peter that he first appears. It is to
Peter that he gives the command to go into Galilee
from Jerusalem, to learn what is required of him and
of the other disciples who remained loyal. And it is to
Peter that Jesus gives the order, "Feed my sheep,"
thus commissioning him and the others to be shep-
herds of God's people.

Other incidents help us to see even more deeply

into Peter's character. The first occurs after Jesus'
arrest and before his execution by hanging on the
cross. Peter remains in the courtyard of the high
priest's house in Jerusalem. There he is accused by a
servant girl of being one of the followers of Jesus.
In a state of desperation, Peter denies the accusation.
Three times he says that he is not one of the band,
even if his accent betrays him as being a Galilean.

Then comes one of the most poignant phrases in
the whole New Testament. It is in Luke's gospel,
which represents Jesus as being nearby. "And the
Lord turned and looked on Peter . . ."

It was the look that broke Peter's heart. He had
three times denied his master whom he loved. "And
he broke down and wept."

The denial and Peter's immediate repentance
were enough to change everything. From that time
forward there was no one firmer in his loyalty, more
certain of his faith, and more devoted to his risen
master's work. The sign of that restoration is in the
fact that Peter was the one to whom the Lord revealed
himself after his crucifixion. As Luke's gospel says,
"The Lord has risen indeed and has appeared to
Simon."

In an incident which is said to have happened before the crucifixion but which reflects what took place
after it, Jesus had prayed urgently for the reestab-

lishment of his disciples' faith. He had said to Peter: "Simon, Simon, behold Satan has asked for you [this is plural and indicates *all* the disciples] in order to sift you like wheat. But I have prayed for thee [this denotes Peter himself] that thy faith may not fail. And when thou [meaning Peter], when thou hast turned again to me, strengthen your brethren." This passage in Luke shows us what did happen. It was Peter who saw the Lord, although others also had this privilege. And it was Peter who "strengthened" them all in their faith.

The final incident, also after the resurrection, is told in John's gospel. The disciples are in Galilee. Peter tells them that he is going fishing, resuming his old trade. Thomas, Nathanael, the two sons of Zebedee, and some others are there, and they say that they will accompany him. They go out in their boat but catch nothing. The next morning they see a stranger on the beach. He tells them to cast their nets once again. They do so and this time they catch an enormous quantity of fish—one hundred and fifty-three, John says. This is important, for the number was a Jewish numerical representation of the whole people. They drag the boat to land, with its heavy burden of fish. And then they see that it is Jesus who has been there and has given them the command to cast their nets once again.

The disciples have a meal with Jesus, eating bread and fish. "When they have finished breakfast, Jesus says to Simon Peter, 'Simon, son of John, do you love me more than these?' "

Peter replies, "Yes, Lord, you know that I love you."

Twice again the question is repeated; twice Peter replies in the same way. Then Jesus says to him, "Feed my sheep," as he had said on each of the other times. But he adds: "When you were young, you girded yourself and walked where you would; but when you are old, you will stretch out your hands and another will gird you and carry you where you do not wish to go." It is a mysterious saying, but the writer of John's gospel gives it this meaning: "This he said, to show by what death Peter was to glorify God."

Written after Peter's martyrdom by crucifixion in Rome, this statement indicates that knowledge of, and veneration for, Peter was widespread in the early Christian community. (Remember that John's gospel probably dates from the turn of the first century.)

These incidents from the four gospels help us to see Peter as he was—warmhearted, impulsive, liable to blurt out things that he might afterward regret. At the same time, he loved his Lord deeply; he was entirely committed to him; he was chosen by him to be the chief of his band of disciples; he was honored by being given the privilege of being the first to know of his resurrection; and he was commanded to "feed the sheep." This was the "rock-man," on whose utter faith Jesus knew that he could safely and securely build a community that would be dedicated to him and to his work in the world. A further demonstration of this fact is seen in Peter's work as a Christian missionary and as one of the two early heads of the Christian Church in Jerusalem. The other was James, "the brother of the Lord"—he has also been called a cousin —who died in Jerusalem many years later.

4

Peter as a Missionary

Dr. Oscar Cullmann, in his excellent study of Peter, ends one section of his book with these words: "The Apostle Peter, in the first period after the death of Jesus, leads the primitive Church in Jerusalem; he then leaves Jerusalem, where the leadership passes over to James; and from then on, by commission of the primitive Church and in dependence upon it, he stands at the head of the Jewish Christian mission."

There, in one sentence, is an admirable summary of what happened in the life of Simon Peter following the crucifixion and resurrection of Christ. The main point is, "he stands at the head of the *Jewish* Christian mission."

The word "Jewish" indicates clearly the distinction between Peter and Paul. Paul became the head of the mission to the Gentile world. Most of his successful work was done in Asia Minor and in Greece. Peter was responsible for the work done in the Jewish world, and particularly in his own native Palestine.

The first reference to Peter as a missionary comes in Acts on the Feast of Pentecost. This was a Jewish festival having to do with the remembrance of events in the past history of the Israelites. Naturally, the first Christians—who were all Jews—would observe it. They were "all together in one place," very likely to share a meal together, as they were accustomed to do with Jesus, whose death had taken place a few days before.

While they were together, they had the strange and overwhelming experience of being possessed by the Spirit. The little company then moved out into the street where they met a number of residents who wondered what all the excitement was about. At this time, Peter delivered his first sermon.

He told the people that he and his friends were by no means drunk or insane, as some suspected. On the contrary, he said, they had just experienced what the ancient prophet Joel had predicted would one day happen: God has poured out his Spirit upon them and they have been empowered by that Spirit.

How did this happen? It was because God had sent his son Jesus, "a man attested to you by God with mighty works and wonders"; and when his own people had put him to death, God "raised him up, having loosed the pangs of death, because it was not possible for him to be held by death." This Jesus, "being therefore exalted at the right hand of God," has poured out on those who had accompanied him during his days in the flesh the Spirit which he had promised to send.

That, said Peter, was what the little band of Christians had experienced. And in that way Jesus had been shown plainly for what he was and is: "Let all the house of Israel therefore know assuredly that God has made him both Lord and Christ, this Jesus whom ye crucified."

The last few phrases are important in order to make sense of what Peter is said to have proclaimed. "Lord" and "Christ": these were the two effective words. We know that "Christ" means the designated and empowered agent of God in bringing in his kingdom. "Lord" is a word that goes along with "Christ." Its significance is that it denotes both one who may be worshiped, since in a profound way he is one with God, and one who is even now present with those who believe in him. In those two words, therefore, Simon Peter stated briefly and succinctly the permanent element in the continuing Christian attitude toward Jesus of Nazareth.

The result of this first speech of Peter's, says Acts, is that those who heard "were cut to the heart." They asked Peter and the others: "Brethren, what then shall we do?"

Peter replied that they should commit themselves in repentance and faith to this same Jesus. Then they should accept baptism. Thus, they, too, would "receive the gift of the Holy Spirit," like the men whom they had observed. God intended that men should thus come to him, "for the promise is to you and to your children, and to all that are far off, every one whom the Lord our God calls to him."

The story goes on to say that many who heard, in fact, did what Peter urged, "and there were added that day about three thousand souls." Those who accepted "the apostles' teaching" became part of their "fellowship" and as such joined in "the breaking of bread and in the prayers" of the Christian community. Furthermore, so impressive was the event that others were attracted to them, "and the Lord added to their number day by day those who were being saved."

This vivid incident shows how the Christian Church began to grow in its very first days, under the leadership of Peter. Scholars have questioned the precise accuracy of the story, and rightly so. In the continued retelling, details were undoubtedly altered.

But as a general picture of what happened, the story is plain enough and may be trusted.

For the next dozen chapters of Acts, the attention of the writer is still centered on Peter, and what he, with his associates, was able to do. There is, for example, the account of the healing of a man "lame from birth," to whom Peter said, "In the name of Jesus Christ of Nazareth, walk." The lame man was made strong and did walk.

There follows still another address by Peter to those who were astonished at this cure. Once again it is a proclamation of Jesus as "Lord" and "Christ," with the plea to repent, accept Jesus, and undergo baptism.

Certain other stories in Acts are significant in respect to Peter's own position and views. One is the story of Ananias and Sapphira, a married couple. Both were Christians, who held back from the community in Jerusalem some of the proceeds which they had received from the sale of property. (The first Christians believed that the things which they possessed were "not their own," but were to be shared as necessary: "they had everything in common." Thus, it was wrong for Ananias and Sapphira to act as they did.) As the leader of the Church, Peter rebuked them. They were both so overwhelmed that they died shortly afterward. A significant aspect of this matter is the way in which

Acts simply assumes that everyone knows that it is Peter who has the authority to act on behalf of his fellow Christians.

In a similar instance, a man called Simon Magus, living in Samaria, claimed to have magical powers. He was interested in the Christian preaching. Peter (along with John) went to Samaria to see him, as well as to further the work of other missionaries there. Simon asked that Peter give to him also the "power of the Holy Spirit," adding that he was willing to pay for this privilege. Again Peter engaged in a terrible rebuke, telling Simon that it was wicked to think that a gift of God could be purchased with money. He urged Simon Magus to repent, lest he come to a fearful end.

This story is interesting not only because it shows Peter exercising authority in the Christian community, but also because it represents him as taking part in one of the very first Christian missions to a territory not entirely Jewish. Simon Peter visited there to confirm those to whom Philip, another early missionary, had brought word of "the kingdom of God and the name of Jesus."

The Samaritan mission was probably undertaken by hellenized Jews. They seemed particularly open to receiving the Christian message, perhaps because they were naturally more ready to entertain ideas which were not conventionally and traditionally Jewish. It is evident that many of them were converted. Saint Stephen, the first Christian martyr, who was stoned to death in Jerusalem, was one of this group. Following his death, a number of his friends fled from the capital city. Very likely they went north to Samaria and sought to win Samaritans to the gospel of Christ.

What attitude did Peter take toward the hellenized Jews? He himself was a loyal Jew, whose conversion to Jesus had not altered his following of traditional Jewish customs. Yet, Peter seems to have taken a mediating position in respect to the hellenized people. He, of course, preferred to continue in the old ways, except that he fervently accepted the messiahship of Jesus. But he was also prepared to fraternize with Jews who were not so meticulous in their observance, once they had become Christians.

Peter's main concern was to hold together in a single community different types of converts to the Christian faith. When James became head of the Jerusalem church, things were different. James was so loyal to his inherited Judaism that he did not see how a person *could* be a Christian without accepting the ancient religion, too.

Jesus himself was a Jew and had kept the Jewish practices in his personal way of life. Did this mean that those who accepted Jesus as Christ and as living

48

Lord must also follow the Jewish customs? Many thought so. But Paul did not. And Peter was quite ready to "eat and drink" with those who were not circumcised—circumcision, for males, was *the* sign of following Jewish ways. Yet, in Peter's desire to keep all Christians in a united fellowship, he did not press the point.

One incident, reported at great length in Acts, concerns the conversion of a Gentile named Cornelius, who was stationed at the town of Caesarea. Cornelius was a member of the Roman army, belonging to a division called "the Italian cohort." He was a "devout man," which means in Acts that he was one of those Gentiles who attended worship in the Jewish synagogue and sought to follow the Jewish Torah. There were many such people in the Roman Empire. The technical term to describe them is "God-fearers" or "devout men." They were Gentiles who were attracted to Judaism largely because of its high moral standards, its insistence on the belief that there is only one God, and the simplicity and purity of Jewish worship.

In the story, Peter had gone to the town of Joppa where he had raised from apparent death a pious Jewish Christian woman named Tabitha (or Dorcas). He remained in Joppa for some time, staying with a Christian Jew whose name was also Simon. While there, Peter had a dream. He saw a great sheet descending from heaven, on which were all manner of "animals, reptiles, and birds of the air." He was ordered to kill some of these and eat. Peter refused, saying that he had never eaten anything "unclean" or "common." But the voice told him three times, "What God has cleansed, you must not call common." What could this dream mean?

Peter soon discovered the meaning. Cornelius, in the not-too-distant town of Caesarea, had also had a dream in which he was told to arrange an interview with "one Simon who is called Peter," who was lodging with Simon in Joppa. Cornelius sent to Joppa to arrange for a meeting; his emissaries arrived the morning after Peter's dream.

Peter went down to Caesarea with some of his friends from Joppa. He met Cornelius, and they talked together for some time. Peter declared the good news about Jesus as the Messiah of God, telling how he had "gone about doing good, healing those that were oppressed by the devil," being put to death, and raised from the dead. He told Cornelius that this Jesus was the one appointed by God. He affirmed that by faith in Jesus men were given the forgiveness of their sins.

While Peter was talking, all those present had an experience like that on the Feast of Pentecost. "The

Holy Spirit fell on all who heard the words," including the Gentiles who were present. As a result, Cornelius and the other Gentiles were ready to be baptized into the Christian fellowship. This Peter did, remaining "for some days" with them in Caesarea.

The interesting thing in this story is that those who were baptized were Gentiles, although they attended Jewish synagogue worship. Peter had learned from his dream that a man's race did not matter, so far as Christian faith is concerned. As he says in Acts, "Truly I perceive that God shows no partiality, but in every nation any one who fears him and does what is right is acceptable to him."

Peter had learned by experience that not only Jews but also Gentiles could be accepted into the Christian Church. They had only to accept Jesus as Messiah and commit themselves to being his followers.

When Peter returned to Jerusalem, he was rebuked by the Jewish Christians there because he had gone "to uncircumcised men and eaten with them." But Peter had his answer ready. He told of his dream, of what had happened as a consequence of it, and of the coming of the Spirit upon both Gentiles and Jews. He ended by saying, "If God gave to *them* [the Gentiles] the same gift as he gave to *us* when we believed in Jesus as Lord and Christ, who was I that I could withstand God?"

His argument was compelling, and the Jewish Christians accepted it. "They glorified God, saying, 'Then to the Gentiles also God has granted repentance unto life.' "

In most Christian thinking, Paul is regarded as the first man to recognize that the Christian faith is not only for those of Jewish race and religion. But it was Peter, not Paul, who first realized the universality of the Christian message. It might even be said that the reason Paul was able to undertake the mission to the Gentiles was because Peter had prepared the way. Otherwise it is hard to see how the Jewish Christians in Jerusalem could have been prepared to assent to Paul's mission, to have empowered him to undertake it, and to have accepted his work gratefully.

One other episode, reported in Acts, is also relevant. This is the account of Peter's imprisonment. He was arrested by Herod, the king in Jerusalem under arrangements with the Roman authorities. James, one of Zebedee's sons, had been killed. This had "pleased the Jews," and Herod decided to continue his persecution. Peter was kept in prison for some time. During this period "earnest prayer for him was made to God" by his fellow believers. The story says that Peter escaped from prison because the iron gate was mysteriously opened for him. He went at once to the place where his friends were praying together. After a brief meeting, Peter "departed and went to another place." That is, he left the holy city of Jerusalem. Where did he go?

No one knows the answer, but a considerable number of scholars think that Peter then went to Rome. Others have said that it was very likely Antioch, since in the letter to the Galatians, Paul speaks of Peter as being in that city. However, Paul gives no mention of the time when Peter was there. One thing is clear, however. Peter's departure from Jerusalem marked the end of his work as the head of the Christian community in that city. His successor was James.

Whether or not Peter went directly to Rome, it is probable that eventually he did go there.

In writing to the Galatians, Paul expressly states that, when he first went to Jerusalem, he went there to do what the Greek text calls "historicizing" Peter. What does Paul mean by that phrase? The usual translation says "visiting Cephas" (or Peter). Why Peter, rather than other Christian figures in Jerusalem? The probable answer is that Peter was accepted as the head of the Christian community in Jerusalem, and, therefore, Paul wished to talk with him.

As for historicizing Peter, however, there is a very sensible answer. "Historicizing" Peter means that Paul, having thus been converted to the "risen and glorified Christ," wished also to hear from Peter's own lips the personal memories which he had about Jesus. Furthermore, since it had been Peter to whom Jesus had first revealed himself after the resurrection, Paul would have wished to know firsthand the sequence of events during those momentous days. Peter was the principal authority.

After these stories in Acts, Peter disappears from history, so far as absolutely certain written evidence is concerned. But this is not the end of his story. The traditions of his time in Rome are too strong to be rejected, even though the tales may be exaggerated.

5

Peter in Rome

Q*uo vadis?*—"Where are you going?" That question, in its Latin form, is the center of an old story that points up the question of Peter's presence and martyrdom in Rome. The tale was expanded into a novel, entitled *Quo Vadis*, written many years ago by the Polish author Henryk Sienkiewicz.

The story concerns the persecution of Christians in the imperial city. When it became very severe, Peter was persuaded, both for his own safety and for the continuing welfare of the Christian Church, that it would be best for him to flee. He made his exit through the gates at the Porta Capena and proceeded down the Via Appia, which leads to the south. As he walked along, he met a stranger who was going toward Rome.

The stranger seemed somehow familiar to Peter, yet he did not recognize him. But it was odd that anybody should be going toward Rome, a city which at that very moment was largely in flames. So Peter asked, "Where are you going?"

The answer came promptly. "I am going to Rome to be crucified afresh."

Then Peter saw that the stranger was Jesus himself, come back to suffer death once more in the imperial city. He would suffer death because his followers, who called themselves by his name, were suffering there. Stricken, Peter turned back toward the city. The stranger vanished; he had been but a vision. Yet Peter knew that the vision was for him. It was a recall to his duty as a Christian to undergo, with other Christians, whatever might await him.

Peter returned to Rome. When he was arrested by Nero's officials, he insisted on being crucified hanging upside down. He wished to be crucified so he might share in his Lord's manner of dying, but felt he was not worthy to die in exactly the same fashion as his Lord had done.

A visitor to Rome today can see the very spot that is thought to have been the place where Peter met the stranger. Of course, it is a story. There is no special reason to think that it actually took place. Yet, it does make two points very clear. The first is that Peter was, indeed, in Rome, with a strong tradition to support it. The second is the understanding it shows of the character of Peter himself. He may have agreed to run away; yet his utter dedication to his Lord was so strong that he had to return and prove his loyalty by death.

Literary sources point to Peter in Rome. Two of them are of special interest because they are relatively early. One is the first letter written by Clement, a Roman Christian, at the end of the first century. It was addressed to fellow Christians in the city of Corinth in Greece.

The Corinthian Christians were in a turmoil. Their worries were centered mainly on the question of who did and did not have authority as leaders of their church. Clement writes a letter to them in which he speaks, among other things, of the "apostolic men," or early leaders of the Christian Church. The date of the letter is generally thought to be A.D. 96.

In the fifth chapter of his letter, Clement writes about Peter, giving his name and saying that "Because of unrighteous jealousy he had to bear not one or two but many torments, and so after he had given his witness he went to the place of glory which was his due." This is an explicit reference, written from Rome itself, of Peter's martyrdom.

Clement also mentions Paul, who was "freed

from the world and went to the holy place" (heaven).
These men, Clement says, "joined a great multitude
of others" who endured persecution. In other words,
Clement is indicating that the Roman Christian community can claim a number of persons, indeed "a
great multitude," who were martyrs for Christ. Fore-
most among them he places Peter and Paul.

The death of Peter could not have taken place
more than about thirty years before Clement writes to
Corinth. Why, therefore, did he not elaborate on his
first reference to Peter, beyond speaking of his death?
Perhaps it was unnecessary to so do, since the story of
Peter's martyrdom was already well known.

The second early source is the letter written by
Saint Ignatius of Antioch to the Christians in Rome,
about the beginning of the second century. Ignatius
had been the head of the Christian congregation in the
Asia Minor city. He had been arrested as a member
of an illegal religion, but had refused to give up his
faith. Now he was on his way to Rome to be executed.
His letter, one of several which he wrote to various
Christian churches, tells the Roman Christians of his
condemnation, urges them not to do anything to inter-
fere with his sentence (he evidently wanted to suffer
martyrdom), and tries to strengthen their own resist-
ance to further persecution.

In his letter, Ignatius wants to make it quite clear

that he is not assuming a dictatorial attitude toward his correspondents. He writes: "Not like Peter and Paul do I give you orders." The point is that he is well aware of the fact that it *was* Peter and Paul who "gave orders" (that is, occupied positions of leadership) in the Roman Church in days gone by. This brief notice is a sign that both of the two great apostles had lived in that city and had been actively engaged in conducting the affairs of the Church there.

Another ancient document which mentions Peter in Rome is the so-called *Ascension of Isaiah*. This early piece of writing attempts to use, in a Christian fashion, some of the recorded incidents in the life of the great Hebrew prophet. In this paper is what Dr. Cullmann calls "the first and earliest document that attests the martyrdom of Peter in Rome." It, too, associates Peter and Paul, and says, "As apostles who were victims of Nero, Peter and Paul are to be taken into account." The date of this work is uncertain. Some place it very early (even in the lifetime of Nero himself—the early sixties of the first century, and hence almost contemporary with the persecution). Others put it much later.

There is other writing that confirms this strong impression of Peter in Rome. For instance, a letter dated about A.D. 170 from Dionysus, as bishop of Corinth, to Christians in Rome, says that both Peter and Paul had taught in Rome and had "borne witness" (i.e., been martyred) there. And in the great, probably earlier, work against heresies by Saint Irenaeus (*Adversus Haereses*), there is a description of the origins of the Christian gospel. Irenaeus states that Peter and Paul had both preached in Rome and had "organized" a church there—a church which is, therefore, to be trusted, because its beginning is with the two greatest of the Christian apostles.

About the year 354, a "deposition," listing the days of death and burial of all bishops known to the time of Sylvester, who died in 335, appeared in Rome. In this and other documents, intended to guide the Christian community in arranging services of worship, Peter is mentioned as first in sequence. With his name is linked that of Paul. The calendar day set aside for the remembrance of the death of the apostles is June 29, although it seems that a date in February was originally designated.

The deposition, called *Depositio Martyrum,* speaks of the martyrdom of Peter as taking place "in the catacombs," and that of Paul on the highway in Ostia, the seaport of Rome.

If, as seems likely from the written evidence, Peter was in Rome, what did he do there? And how did his death occur?

The Christian community in Rome was composed very largely, at the beginning, of Greek-speaking Jews. There may have been as many as fifty thousand Jews in the city, but not many would have become Christians. There were also Gentile converts, either from among the God-fearers or from among those who had been attracted by the lives of the Christians or by the proclamation of Jesus Christ as the Lord.

Peter, as a distinguished Christian leader and one who had been an eyewitness to the events of Jesus' life on earth, would have received honor from all these persons. He would have presided at their "breaking of bread"; he would have preached and taught; and he would have shared in the general administration of the church. Being the man he was, Peter would have been energetic and vigorous, taking forthright stands on many issues. Since he could understand both the Jewish and the Gentile ways of seeing things, he surely would have been a reconciling factor in the life of the small community of Christians.

Peter's relations with Paul, who was in Rome but under "house arrest," are not known. Since both of them frequently urged that Christians should live in brotherly concord with one another, there probably was no controversy between them. The Harvard historian George LaPiana theorized that in a city as large as Rome, with so many different areas or sections, there were almost certainly a number of Christian congregations. This would have been increasingly true as the number of converts increased.

Different groups of Christians would meet regularly at different houses. These groups would naturally have the same faith, worship in the same way, and have frequent contact with each other. But they would be distinct, with their own organizations and boards of elders. It would be natural for Peter to be directly concerned with one group or groups, and for Paul to be responsible for others.

The city of Rome was ruled by Nero, a tyrannical man, a sensualist, and a complete egotist. He built for himself an enormous "Golden Palace," which was never completed. Its foundations and some of its magnificent rooms are still visited by tourists. He spent money without end, and in order to obtain what he wanted, he was prepared to go to almost any lengths. He had no regard for his family, poisoning those whom he disliked or who, to his mind, were plotting against him.

One of the more spectacular things that Nero did, if the historians are correct, was to have a hand in starting a fire that destroyed a large section of the great, crowded, and, in parts, ramshackle city. The citizens were understandably furious. They did not like Nero anyway, and they believed that he had decided to start the fire "just to make a Roman holiday" for himself.

In an effort to find somebody to blame for the disaster, Nero and his advisers decided to "take it out" on the Christians. Jews were not popular in Rome; Christian Jews were even less so. But Gentile Christians were regarded as possible traitors to the state. Therefore, it was easy enough to make the Christian community the scapegoat. And this Nero did. Roman historians say explicitly that this was Nero's plan and that he carried it out.

Naturally, those who were known to occupy positions of importance in the Christian churches were among the first to be arrested and put to death. This would include Peter and Paul, by all odds the outstanding Christians in the city. And so they were killed.

Dr. Walter Lowrie (see bibliography) writes that, in his opinion, with considerable archaeological and other material to build on, Peter and Paul were later buried in the same grave. The Christians in Rome then honored both apostles as *their* saints. But they gave priority to Peter, remembering that he had been the accepted head of the early Christian community in Rome. He, not Paul, had been a companion of Jesus'; he, not Paul, had both denied his Lord and had been restored by his Lord to a place of service. And it was to Peter to whom the Lord said: "Feed my sheep."

Peter had given the remaining years of his life to "feeding the sheep." He had suffered death because of his faithfulness. Small wonder that the Christians in Rome gave him preeminence. Small wonder that the continuing Christian Church, in Rome and elsewhere, is prepared to call him "the prince of the apostles."

6

Letters Attributed to Peter

The two letters in the New Testament which are attributed to Peter are relatively short as compared with the long and complicated ones written by Paul. In the Revised Standard Version, the first of the Petrine epistles takes up only three and a half pages. The second is just two pages long.

These two documents are quite straightforward and clear, both in language and in development of ideas. They are marked by simplicity of style and obvious meaning. Traditionally, First Peter (the first letter) is taken to be a "baptismal tractate"—a discussion in letter form of the meaning and the consequences of baptism. The message of Second Peter is to strengthen Christian believers against dangerous and heretical opinions, and to urge patience because the long-expected "return" of Jesus—which all early Christians thought would occur within a short time—had not yet taken place.

Scholars have asked whether these two letters were really written by Peter. The general conclusion seems to be that the second letter is most certainly not from Peter himself. Its subjects, references, and theological position place it in a period very much later than Peter's own lifetime. Some scholars say it was written in the early second century; others put it somewhat earlier, but still regard it as one of the last written books of the New Testament.

Scholarly opinion is divided about the first letter. The majority of experts think that it was not actually written by Simon Peter himself. A "faithful brother" named Silvanus is mentioned at the end of the letter as an amanuensis—a secretary expressing in writing ideas given him by another. Some say that Silvanus, presumably a Christian teacher toward the latter part of the first century, actually wrote the letter under the name of Peter, to give it prestige and to honor a revered Christian leader. Another view is that the letter contains Petrine ideas and teaching, but was written by somebody else, with Peter's authority. In that case, it could have been prepared during the last year of Peter's life. Still another theory is that the letter is a churchly document having to do with the nature and results of Christian baptism, from the late first century or early second, to which have been added the first and last few verses in which Peter is named. And yet another opinion is the one that was simply taken for granted for many years: this is, indeed, a letter written by Peter himself. However, it is hard to see how an unschooled man like Simon Peter could have written in such very good Greek—the style and language of this letter are among the very best in the whole New Testament.

Whoever was the author, there is no reason to assume that the actual contents of the letter are not Peter's thoughts. On the contrary, granted the importance attached to baptism in the Christian Church from its very first days and the way in which the letter represents the significance of Jesus, there is every reason to assume that what is said in it is what Peter himself would have thought.

First Peter begins with the usual opening style of a letter written in the Graeco-Roman world—an anouncement of the author and a statement of the recipient, or recipients, followed by an introductory salutation. "Peter, an apostle of Jesus Christ, to the exiles of the dispersion in Pontus, Galatia, Cappadocia, Asia, and Bithynia, chosen and destined by God the Father and sanctified by the Spirit for obedience to Jesus Christ and for sprinkling with his blood: May grace and peace be multiplied to you." The list of places has importance. They are all in Asia Minor, an area that Peter must have visited. But the letter goes on at once to a discussion of its main theme.

The discussion continues until the statement that this letter is "by Silvanus," with a reference to its having come from the Church "at Babylon." Surely that does not mean the once great city of Babylon, in the Tigris-Euphrates valley, but rather the city of Rome. In the last book of the New Testament, "The Revelation of Saint John the Divine," the name "Babylon" is used consistently to indicate the capital of the Roman Empire.

The baptismal discussion begins with an explicit reference to the rite, speaking of Christians as "born anew to a living hope"—rebirth was the usual way in which baptism was regarded. This rebirth, it is said, comes through a participation in the life of Jesus Christ, "raised from the dead." Although the greater number of Christian believers have never actually "seen him," they know him through their "belief," which has brought them "unutterable and exalted joy."

The writer emphasizes that as "newborn babes," Christians must long for "pure spiritual milk," so that they may "grow up to wholeness." Those who have been baptized, he says, have become "chosen and precious" in God's sight. Then he tells them that they are "living stones" in a new "spiritual house," sharers in a "holy priesthood," because through Christ they have become a "chosen race, a royal priesthood, a holy nation, and God's own people," who are to "declare the wonderful deeds of him who called them out of darkness into his marvelous light." In consequence, their duty is to "abstain from the passions of the flesh," to maintain "good conduct," to "live as free men without using their freedom as a pretext for evil."

The letter then spells out in detail what this will imply. It speaks, for example, about servants as those who should be obedient to their masters, although it also urges masters to be gentle and understanding to their servants. In this connection, something of Peter's theology comes out, for the author notes that Christ also lived as an obedient servant to God, finally "bearing our sins in his own body on the tree [the cross]," so that those who believed in him "might die to sin and live to righteousness." Wives and husbands are urged to be understanding one of the other. And all Christians, of whatever rank or position, are to have "unity of spirit, sympathy, love of the brethren, a tender heart and a humble mind."

Baptism itself is then compared to the cleansing of the body. It is pointed out that this is no mere physical washing but an "appeal to God for a clear conscience" so that the baptized may live acceptably with God and men. It is said that every Christian has the obligation to "make a defense to anyone who asks," respecting "the hope that is in them"—that is, they are to speak of their faith and be prepared to defend it.

Finally, the writer says that "the end of all things is at hand." He is referring, of course, to the belief then held that very shortly Christ would return from heaven to earth. When he returned, "the end," or last days of the world, would take place and the "final judgment" would occur. In the meantime, Christians above all—those who are of "the household of faith," as the author calls them—should "entrust their souls to a faithful Creator," living in faith and humility even when called to undergo suffering through persecution or because of the "evil-speaking" about them which comes from the non-Christian outsider. They have the confidence that "the God of all grace, who has called them to his eternal glory in Christ, will himself restore, establish, and strengthen them" to face any and every trial and trouble.

Thus, the first of the letters attributed to Peter is a moving exhortation to Christian believers to live lives of love, understanding, and peace. They must show by their daily conduct and their attitude to others that they have been brought into a family where the love of God shown in Christ is the ruling factor.

They must be brave no matter what persecution or difficulty they may be called upon to face.

The thrust of the letter is toward a life in love, such as Christians ought always to live. Circumstances may alter, conditions may change, but that main drive can still continue as the central motif of Christian life. That is what the letter wishes to make clear.

In the second letter, the theme is also Christian life in the world, but this time the stress is on the patience that must be shown because the return of Christ is delayed. The recipients are reminded that "with the Lord one day is as a thousand years, and a thousand years as one day." Human time scales are not the same as God's. Hence, men should accept what seems to them a strange delay in the promised return when "a new heaven and a new earth" will be established. In the meanwhile, they are to live "in holiness and godliness."

The writer says that there are those who deny or misrepresent the truth of the Christian gospel, turning it into "cleverly devised myths." These men were the so-called "gnostics" toward the end of the first century. They tried to make Christianity a religious cult filled with strange talk about emanations from God, hidden truths which only especially spiritual people could grasp, and unchristian ideas of conduct. Teaching like that must be rejected, says the author,

71

since it makes complete nonsense of the gospel that was preached by those who had known Jesus and who were genuinely loyal to him and his intentions.

The letter ends with a plea for stability in the faith on the part of all who profess the name of Christ as their Master and Lord. It is a very brief document, but it was written specifically with the problems of contemporary Christians in mind. The purpose of the letter is clear: steadfastness in faith, patience in tribulation, conduct that reflects the love of God in Christ, and bravery in maintaining the things that the Christian community believed and taught.

There is also a comment in this letter on Paul's teaching. The writer says that "our beloved brother Paul wrote to you according to the wisdom given him, speaking of this as he does in all his letters; yet there are some things in them hard to understand, which the ignorant and unstable twist to their own destruction . . ." Many who have studied Saint Paul's writings will agree with this author that in those writings there are, indeed, "some things . . . hard to understand."

These two letters are a good indication of what Christians were thinking during the second half of the first century. The very fact that they are attributed to Peter himself, even if incorrectly, shows that he was regarded as an authority. At the same time nobody would have had him say things that were entirely alien to what he taught during his own ministry. Thus, they are of value in giving a rough idea of how Peter must have regarded baptism, the nature of Christian life, the problems faced by believers, and the necessity for loyalty and courage on the part of his fellow Christians.

7

The Church and Christian Faith

We have read of the life of Peter. What of the life of the early Christian Church which he served? What sort of community did his leadership, and that of the other first Christian apostles, bring into being?

Some of what is known about the early Church comes from the New Testament itself, which provides not only facts but also a setting for the facts. Other source material includes the very few but helpful remarks which non-Christians made about Christianity. Roman historians like Tacitus and Suetonius, letter writers like the great Roman governor Pliny, Jewish writers like Josephus, can be of use in this area. Within the Christian Church itself, there is also helpful material. Some of it is a little later than the early Church

—about A.D. 50 to the end of the first century—but it is indicative of earlier days.

In the middle of the first century, or shortly after, there were Christians in Palestine, of course, but there were also Christian congregations in many places throughout the Mediterranean area, such as Asia Minor, Greece, and in Rome. The number is not known, but they must have been in the several thousands by this time. For the most part, they were in cities or large towns. This is why even today we sometimes speak of non-Christians as "pagans." It is simply the ancient word for countrypeople—people who, because they lived in fairly remote spots, had not yet been reached by early Christian missionaries.

What sort of people made up the Christian communities? On one occasion Paul speaks of "not many mighty and not many noble" folk. This would suggest that the converts were for the most part simple people, very likely from the lower middle class and from the city proletariat. Large numbers were Jews who had been converted to the new faith. Others were from among the God-fearers. Some would have been natives of the cities where Christian faith was preached, drawn by the honesty, decency, kindness, and even love shown by Christians.

Some evidence suggests that a few—doubtless a

very few—people of higher social status and better education had joined the Christian Church. Some references seem to show that even a few members of the imperial family and court in Rome had become Christian, especially one woman of the Flavian family. But it was only during the second century that intellectuals were brought into the Christian faith in any large numbers—men like Justin Martyr, a philosopher, for example.

Certainly the great majority of Christians, for the first half century at least, were just what Paul said—neither "noble" nor "mighty." They were people with small incomes, artisans, craftsmen, as well as slaves and servants and underprivileged men and women in the slums of the great cities. A hundred years or more afterward, this was still largely the case. This is why Celsus, an early opponent of Christianity, wrote that the Church was composed mainly of ignorant, unlearned, poor, and "worthless" people.

In a response to Celsus, Origen, the great Alexandrine Christian theologian, rejoiced in this fact. He wrote seventy years or so after Celsus' book, but he was ready to acknowledge that the charge might still be made. He considers the fact to be an indication of God's own kindness and care for his human children, since it shows that God loves everybody, perhaps especially the poor and ignorant, even if he does not reject those who are clever, learned, or financially and socially well-placed.

The little Christian communities held their meetings in the houses of the members. Church buildings did not exist, nor would they have been permitted to exist under the Roman regulations about religious cults. Christianity was regarded as a forbidden sect, although some Christians tried to urge that it be made legal since it posed no threat to the peace and stability of the empire. One of the purposes of Luke's gospel was probably to make just such a plea. But during that early period, Christianity was illegal. Hence, its meeting places were secret.

Many people think that the catacombs at Rome were dug out by Christians as places for their secret meetings. This is incorrect. The word "catacomb" originally had no reference to Christian places of meeting. Neither did it originally refer to cemeteries, Christian or otherwise. It comes from a Greek term, *cumbe*, which means a depression in the ground. By adding the preposition *kata* (which means "in the place of" or "at"), the word becomes "catacomb."

The first known catacomb is at the Church of San Sebastiano near Rome, and the locality, beyond the third milestone on the Via Appia, was known as *ad Catacumbas*. Probably there was a narrow ravine near what is now the church. In the course of time, some

Romans were buried—or rather, their ashes were placed—there. Then, by association, any place of burial received the same name. And eventually, by popular usage, the word described specifically Christian burial places located in the many long tunnels dug under the earth at places in and near Rome.

Christians did meet in the catacombs, but only to bury their dead and to "break bread" in memory of the dead. But their regular places of meeting were in private houses. Since they were poor, the houses would not have been very grand. If there happened to be a member who was better off than the others, he made his house available to the community. This is why we read in Paul's letters of "the church at so-and-so's house."

For what purpose did the Christians meet? Primarily they met to share together in what they called "the breaking of the bread" or what today we call the Holy Communion, the Eucharist, or the Mass. It is a little misleading to use these terms, however, since they suggest the formalized, or stylized, kind of worship familiar in modern churches. The early Christians had a much less formal worship service.

Very early Christian believers often liked to call their worship the *agape*. That is a Greek word which means "love." To use the word about the rite of "breaking of bread" was to speak of it as a meal at which Christian love was expressed in a common eating of bread and drinking of wine. In doing so, the participants experienced the presence of their Lord, who himself was believed to be God's love embodied in a human personality. They followed the example of Jesus at his last supper with his disciples, before his crucifixion. They took bread, which they broke and shared together, the bread having been offered to God in a prayer of thanksgiving: "Blessed are you, Lord God of the universe, for giving us bread to strengthen our lives."

Then they may have eaten a regular evening meal together. At the conclusion they set apart a cup containing wine mixed with water—people in the ancient world were accustomed to dilute their wine with some water—and all drank from the cup, which had also been blessed by a thanksgiving: "Blessed are you, Lord God of the universe, for giving us wine to make glad man's heart." This was what Jesus and his disciples had done.

Scholars think that the Christian churches gradually decided to unite the bread and wine parts into one rite, reserving the common meal until afterward. In any event, the purpose of the meetings, held on "the first day of the week," was to observe this act of worship. It is significant that it was on Sunday and not on the Jewish holy day, the Sabbath, or Saturday (the seventh day). The reason for this was that Christians believed that Jesus had appeared as risen from the dead on the first day of the week. Since they were holding their worship in order to realize his presence with them as their risen Lord, it was appropriate to observe the rite on the day when tradition said that he had risen.

In association with the breaking of bread, letters from other Christian groups were read, prayers were offered, and an address was given. The service was held at night; only later did it take place in the early morning. Being gathered together in this fashion, the Christians experienced a tremendous sense of fellowship and friendship, and it was unthinkable that any faithful believer should absent himself from the regular breaking of bread or the agape. Indeed, if somebody was cut off from participation, it was real "excommunication"—refusal of the right to "communicate" or share in the meal. That was regarded as the very worst punishment that could be meted out to any Christian guilty of some very serious fault.

As a leader Peter would "preside," as was said. The term for what now is called the "celebrant of the Mass (the priest)" was then "the president." He was the one who said the prayers, and blessed and distributed the sacred elements of bread and wine. The president sat in the middle on one side of the table, which was covered by a large white cloth. He faced his fellow Christians, and beside him sat the other officials of the local group.

The structure of these first Christian congregations was very simple. The president and the elders, or senior men, formed a kind of steering committee, charged with administration and (among other things) seeing to it that the poor and needy were cared for, the sick visited, the dead buried, and other pastoral duties performed. Very likely the apostles did not always remain in one place. They would go from congregation to congregation, binding together the scattered Christian groups in parts of a city or in one whole area of the known world. In this way, they were like present-day bishops. In fact, some experts think that today's bishops are the descendants of such "apostolic men."

While the apostles, the local leaders, and local elders were very much in charge of the work of the Church, the ordinary Christian member (a "layman") had his share in the work. Because he was a member of the Church, he shared in what the First Letter of Saint Peter called the "royal priesthood." That meant that he shared in the life of Jesus Christ himself. The division of clergy from laity, so familiar today, was not known. Nor were the clergy themselves divided into bishops, priests, deacons, or subdeacons. To be the president of a local congregation, or to be one of the elders, or senior men, was both an honor and a responsibility. It was only later, perhaps around the turn of the first century, that the sort of divisions which are found today held any real importance.

Christians had not yet developed a tightly knit system of doctrines or dogmas. They held firmly to certain basic convictions, but they had not as yet had time to work these out in detail. They were convinced believers in the one and only God, the God of the Jewish people. He was the creator of the world, and it was he whose purpose was being worked out both in nature and in history. His character was like that of a loving father, although his love could be stern and demanding. To call God "father" did not mean to think of him as easygoing or sentimental. The idea of fatherhood, both in Judaism and elsewhere, was a combination of love and the demand that his children do the good and right and just thing.

The Christian was distinguished from others who believed in God by his conviction that God had sent Jesus Christ into the world, so that God's children might receive the forgiveness of sins, the power to live according to the divine will, and a promise of eternal life with God beginning now and continuing after death. Such early Christian teachers as Paul claimed this to mean that Jesus was indeed a true and genuine human being, but that he was also something more—and the "something more" was the centrally important thing about him. In him and through him, God had acted. "In Christ God was reconciling the world to himself." Those are Paul's words, but Peter, in the sermons at the beginning of the Acts of the Apostles, says exactly the same thing in his own way. Thus, it could be said that Jesus is the man in whom God acted in history in a very special way. He could be called "divine," for the act of God in him was nothing other than the very reality of God the Creator.

Sharing these two beliefs, and knit together with others in the Christian community, the believer found himself caught up in a new kind of life which was "the fellowship of the Holy Spirit." The tremendous vigor of his Christian faith, the deep significance of his common life with others, and the strengthening power which he felt to live in obedience to God's purpose were all the "gifts" of the Holy Spirit. That is, they were the working in him of God himself. Saint Paul put these three together in one familiar verse which we call "The Grace." "The grace of our Lord Jesus Christ, the love of God, and the fellowship of the Holy Spirit."

But there was something more in the Christian faith. The cross and the resurrection were at its heart; they made all the difference. Jesus had been "the suffering Servant of God," willing to die if it were God's will, as he believed it was. In consequence of that death on the cross, a new openness between God and man had been established. This had been confirmed and validated when God "raised Jesus from the dead," thus showing that he had, indeed, made his crucified servant "both Lord and Christ." Through the resurrection of the one who had accepted death, Christians could know that that same one was indeed the Messiah whom many Jews had expected to come. They could also know him as still present with them as their "living Lord."

What it meant to be a Christian in the very earliest days of the Church may be summed up in three points:

First, it meant living in charity or in love. It was said in those days, by outsiders, "See how these Christians love one another." When a later Christian writer repeats this, he suggests that the words now have an ironical ring. Perhaps that was true at a later date. But during the early days, it was meant sincerely. Christians did love one another.

Second, the loyalty of believers was noteworthy. Very few deserted the Church. Their life together was so strong, with such deep concern for common goals, that people did not wish to deny what had given them a purpose in life. This loyalty was expressed in their weekly meetings of worship. It was shown in their helpfulness to each other. It was also shown in their readiness to suffer persecution and death, rather than to deny their faith in Jesus as their Lord and Master. Many of them were called upon to undergo just that penalty for their membership in the Christian Church. There must have been thousands who died, either by the sword or by being thrown to the lions in the Roman arenas, or in some other way. Sometimes they were sent as prisoners to work in salt mines. This was a terrible fate, with great privation and pain. But in some salt mines in Sicily, where Christians labored as slaves, there has been found scratched on the walls the Latin word *vita*, "life." Even under such appalling conditions, the workers still felt that they were sharers in the "life" which (as they were convinced) they had been given through their faith in Jesus and their membership in the Christian Church.

Finally, the life of the Christian was marked by what seemed to their fellow citizens to be astounding sexual purity. In that period, the sexual morality in many parts of the Graeco-Roman world was very lax, even licentious. Some cities, like Corinth, were noted for sexual excess and perversion. Even in Rome itself, standards had declined to such an extent that Emperor Caesar Augustus, some decades earlier, had been obliged to enact stringent laws to preserve some show of decency among the leaders in his court and the members of the Roman aristocracy. If that were the case at higher levels, what must have been the situation elsewhere?

But Christians were different. Their sexual morality was high. They honored marriage; they condemned promiscuous sexual relations; they rejected sexual perversions. Perhaps as much as any other single thing, this aspect of Christian character attracted attention and won respect. A Roman governor such as Pliny can find only praise to give to the Christians in this respect, although he regards their "singing hymns to Christ as to a god" as being rather silly. He did not realize the connection of these two things—it was precisely because Christians worshiped a Lord who was himself the embodiment of moral virtue that they were impelled and strengthened to live such lives themselves.

Perhaps this picture of the first Christian Church seems overidyllic. But Christians *were* different, both in personal conduct and in belief and worship. It was only in the fourth century and thereafter, when the Christian Church was "established" as the official religion of the Roman state, that the gap between profession and practice began to widen. But in the early days, this was not so.

In respect to Jesus himself, some scholars think

they can prove that Peter was the first to explain the significance of Jesus in terms of the "Suffering Servant" figure prophesied in the Old Testament book we call Isaiah. In that prophet there is the portrayal of one whom God will use, through the suffering he undergoes, to bring salvation to men. In Peter's speeches in Acts, this is the way that he interprets the meaning of Jesus' death on the cross. Dr. Cullmann says: "The christology of the apostle Peter . . . [was] dominated by the concept of 'The Servant of God.' If so, he who tried to turn Jesus from the way of suffering and denied him at the decisive moment of the Passion story, was the first one who, after Easter, grasped the necessity of this offense."

Peter came to see that the way to resurrection was by the path of crucifixion. That is, that only by dying for the sake of men could Jesus bring life and forgiveness to those men.

Once again, Peter was vividly aware of the reality of the Holy Spirit. On the Feast of Pentecost he himself had experienced this gift. So also, when he had talked with the Roman centurion Cornelius, he had witnessed that same gift coming even to Gentiles. And when he went to Samaria on behalf of the Jerusalem Church, the story says that once more the Holy Spirit "came upon" those who were converted to Jesus as the Messiah. Thus, in Peter's "theology" may be included a strong conviction about the Holy Spirit as the working of God in men's hearts and lives to enable them to respond to the proclamation of Jesus Christ.

In other ways, evidently, Peter held the common faith of the Christian Church of his time. And there is no doubt that his convictions in regard to moral teaching were not only identical with but also helped to mold the position that characterized the early Christian fellowship.

8

Head of the Church

No Christian of whatever denomination would think of anyone but Jesus Christ himself as the "head of the Church." On the other hand, the title is accurate for Peter, too, in terms of the human leadership of the Christian world. Saint Peter has been regarded as the human "head of the Church," its leader, its teacher, and its chief representative.

Many non-Roman Catholics have the idea that the Roman Church wishes to claim the pope as the one and only head of the Church. But this is nonsense. No Roman Catholic, no Roman Catholic theologian, and above all, no bishop of Rome, has ever hinted that the man who is chosen by the College of Cardinals to be the pope is a substitute for the Lord Jesus Christ. On the contrary, the most loved title given to the pope is not, in fact, the official one of "chief pontiff." In Latin he is called *servus servorum Dei*, "the servant of the servants of God."

Since Jesus Christ was the fulfillment of Isaiah's prophecy of the coming of "the Suffering Servant," and thought of as "the Servant of God," this title for the pope is very revealing. It represents a continuation of the insight of Peter himself: that the real glory and wonder of God is not seen in earthly splendor but in humble service of God toward and for his human children. As the one who is Peter's successor as leader of the Church in Rome, the pope appropriately is known as "the servant" of those men who know themselves *all* to be "servants of God."

Every visitor to Rome is likely to see elaborate ceremonies in which the pope takes part. He is carried on a special chair through Saint Peter's. He sits on a throne behind the high altar at the far eastern end of the great building, and there is much to-do about his activities. But all these are not religiously significant customs. They are remnants of an old cultural pattern that goes far back in the history of Western civilization, to the days when the bishop of Rome was the only bulwark left against pagan invasion and destruction of Christian values.

Of necessity, the pope was forced to take upon

himself civil as well as spiritual duties, if Western Christian culture was to be preserved. It is noteworthy, too, that recent popes—above all, John XXIII and his successor, Paul VI—have been anxious to reduce or abolish most of this splendor and ceremonial magnificence. Thus, in the last quarter century or so, the ceremonies at Saint Peter's have been shorn of much of their earthly magnificence. The pope himself has appeared more among the faithful as a humble, loving, and devoted "servant of the servants of God."

The position of "servant of God" began with Jesus' words to Peter: "You are Rock, and upon this Rock I will build my Church." What did Jesus actually mean by the words?

It seems, at first glance, as though Jesus meant that Peter was as firm and strong as a rock, and that it was upon that firmness and strength that the Christian community of faith and life would be built. But it is not quite so simple as that. Even in the first three or four centuries of the Christian Church, there was much discussion of Jesus' meaning, and opinion was divided into two schools. One said that it was, indeed, Peter's own firmness and strength that constituted the foundation of the Christian Church. The other said that it was firmness and strength of the sort that Peter showed (but not necessarily his own manifestation of these) which was the foundation. One group emphasized *Peter's* faith; the other Peter's *faith*.

This disagreement as to meaning has continued through the centuries. In the years since the Christian Church as a whole was divided into separate churches, the disagreement has tended to become a matter of what particular group one belonged to. Roman Catholics have stressed the *first* meaning—it was *Peter's* faith that was intended; Protestants have stressed the second—it was Peter's *faith* which Jesus meant. Eastern Orthodox Christians have been divided, some taking one position and some the other. This disagreement has often been accompanied by bitter controversy, and, in consequence, the real importance of Peter has largely been forgotten by Protestants. Only in quite recent years has there been a willingness to see that Simon Peter was, indeed, the chief of the band of Jesus' disciples. On the other hand, some Roman Catholic writers have made exaggerated claims for Peter, claims for which there is no historical evidence and which today the best scholars frankly disavow.

However, it is possible for the two positions to be reconciled. The way to do so is to recognize that what a man is cannot be separated from what he does. What a man is includes what he believes and thinks and does. A person is what he commits himself to, engages in, and performs.

If this is the case, then *Peter's* faith and Peter's *faith* are inseparable. What Jesus was saying was neither that Peter, as an isolated person, was the one and only "rock" on which he would build the Church, nor that the faith which Peter had just boldly professed, quite separated from the man who professed it, was the "rock." What Jesus was saying was that "Peter with his faith" was the "rock."

Even more significant, that is exactly what did happen. The risen Lord Jesus appeared first to Peter, who then "strengthened his brethren," as Luke's gospel says. Peter was the spokesman for the very first Christian community on that Feast of Pentecost when so many were converted after his sermon. It is impossible to separate Peter from that rocklike faith or to separate that rocklike faith from Peter.

As Dr. Cullmann states: "The fact remains that when Jesus says that he will build his *ecclesia* [church] upon this rock, he really means the person of Simon. Upon this disciple, who in the lifetime of Jesus possessed the specific advantages and the specific weaknesses of which the gospels speak, upon him who was then their spokesman, their representative in good as well as in bad, and in this sense was the rock of the group of the disciples—upon him is to be founded the Church, which after the death of Jesus will continue his work upon earth." Thus, essentially "the Roman Catholic exegesis [interpretation of the meaning] must be regarded as correct . . ."

Does that correctness, however, also mean that the successors of Peter (the popes) possess exactly the same authority and centrality as Peter himself was given? How did such an idea arise?

We do not know whether Peter himself first established the Christian group, or groups, in Rome. But we can be reasonably sure that when he went there he continued his work as preacher, teacher, and a chief administrator. The Christian community did continue in Rome, despite the persecutions that afflicted it.

But Rome was the capital city of the whole Roman Empire, which at that time extended from what is now Iran and Iraq westward to the Atlantic, encompassing the entire Mediterranean basin and all the lands surrounding it. It reached north from northern Africa to include the major portion of Great Britain. In the northeast it included vast areas reaching to the Danube River and beyond and a good portion of modern Germany. Obviously, Rome was an important place; in fact, the *most* important place in the known world. And the dignity which belonged to the imperial city, in a secular way, was naturally attached to the Christian Church there.

There were other great Christian centers during the next few centuries, places like Jerusalem, Antioch, Alexandria. But Rome was central and a city to which people went, if for no other reason than for trade and for the carrying on of governmental business. If they were Christians, they would look for their fellow believers in the city. They would worship with them, talk with them, perhaps remain in their homes as guests—Christians were well known for their hospitality and their readiness to entertain other Christians. In this way, the habit grew of turning to the Christian Church in the city of Rome for guidance on matters of faith, churchly organization, and the conduct of worship.

The fact that Peter and Paul had lived in Rome and had been martyred there added to the prestige of the Christian Church in the city. The way in which the Roman Christians resisted the "heresies," or false teachings of various thinkers, and stood firm for the faith increased that prestige. If one wished to find a place where the faith, as the first apostles had preached it, was maintained with vigor, then Rome was the place to go.

In *Against the Heresies*, Saint Irenaeus speaks of

the need to appeal to the testimony of the apostles. He mentions the various churches in the world where this testimony is faithfully remembered. Then he speaks of the church in Rome as "the very ancient and universally known church founded and organized by Peter and Paul." In saying that the church in Rome was "founded" by Paul, Irenaeus is certainly wrong. But the real point of his reference comes in a further statement when he says that since Rome is the place where everybody goes, it is also the place where Christians can go to learn what is the *true* Christian faith. Why? Because it is to the church in Rome that "all resort."

There is another of those troublesome pieces of scholarly investigation. The phrase that Irenaeus uses is in Latin. It says that everybody "resorts to Rome." The Latin may be translated as meaning one of two things: Rome is the place where people go, in the sense of visiting it; or Rome is the place to which people appeal, in the sense of asking advice or guidance. If the latter is his meaning, Irenaeus is saying something like, "If you want to know what the truth is, go to (resort to) John Jones, for he is an expert in this matter." The probability is that Irenaeus intended the second meaning ("go to Rome for expert advice") because he knew that the first meaning was taken for granted.

And that is the point.

During the period when the Roman Empire was still in existence, with the emperor living in the city of Rome and the administration headquarters located there, it was natural and inevitable that the Christian Church in the city should be highly important for all Christians everywhere. This was true theologically as well as in other ways.

When later the imperial city fell on evil days and the old empire was in ruins, the remaining historical figure in the city was the Christian bishop. The empire had become Christian some time before, when Emperor Constantine made the Christian faith the "official belief" of the Roman world. Now, with no emperor and no civil government in Rome, the only thing left to hold things together was the bishop. As it happened, the men who held office as bishop during this time were of great stature, able to do exactly what the circumstances required. They kept things in order; they maintained the stability of government, so far as this was possible; and they did all in their power to provide for the citizenry who were impoverished, badly frightened, and almost in danger of destroying themselves in their horror at the loss of the former dignity and glory of the Roman capital.

Finally, Rome was the place where the shrine of Saint Peter was situated and where the memory of the great apostle was unfailingly preserved. Rome and its bishop were linked with the memory of Saint Peter and his martyrdom. To say the word "Rome" was to bring to mind the figure of Saint Peter.

By a very natural—indeed, inevitable—development, the man who, in succession to Peter, was the leader of the church in Rome became the man who was literally the successor of Peter. To be "in succession to Peter" might mean only to be the person who held much the same sort of office and did much the same sort of work as Simon Peter had done centuries before. But to be "the successor of Peter" could mean, and soon did come to mean, to be the one who enjoyed the same position, in respect to the whole Christian Church, that Peter himself almost certainly had occupied during his days in Rome before his death.

Whether or not that development was sound is unimportant. Certainly the Christian faith would very likely have vanished from the earth if there had not been, in the capital city of the Roman Empire and in the days after the empire's collapse in the fifth century, a Christian community that held fast to Peter's faith, with a leader who was revered by fellow believers throughout the world.

9

The Excavations in Rome

Most everyone seems to be interested in archaeological discoveries. Newspapers and periodicals publish articles and reproduce photographs of "finds" made in excavations, or "diggings," and many books show the pictures of what has been discovered.

This is natural, since somehow it makes ancient people come alive when we can see, and perhaps touch, the utensils they used and the walls of the houses where they lived, and put our feet on the very streets they once walked. This explains why so many thousands of visitors to Rome spend much time walking through the now-excavated ruins of the old Roman Forum and enjoy excursions into the various catacombs which have been opened for public inspection.

One of the most exciting and interesting series of

excavations ever undertaken has been going on for years underneath the great church of Saint Peter's in Rome. When the team of archaeologists announced that they had opened up a cavelike room that might have been the final burial place of Peter himself, there was almost wild excitement—in Rome, of course, but elsewhere as well. And when, most recently, the Vatican authorities said that there was practically no doubt that this *was* the traditional shrine and that possibly some of the bones discovered there were, in truth, the bones of Peter, the enthusiasm was endless.

Unquestionably, it has been disclosed through various excavations that there were burials *ad Catacumbas*. In later times that church (San Sebastiano) served as the grave of Saint Sebastian, whose legend is well-known in Rome. The excavations have revealed that at this place, during the first century, there was a Roman villa or country house. It has also been shown that at this spot, in what is volcanic stone, there was a quarry. Furthermore, in the depression were discovered *columbaria*, graves in which the cremated ashes of the dead were placed. Finally, there was a room called a *triclia*, a place where evidently a cult of some kind was carried out.

The old legend said that Damasus, an early Christian bishop in Rome, had erected in that place a church where "the bodies of the holy Apostles Peter and Paul had rested." From the wall scratchings in that spot it is known that, some time before A.D. 260, the practice of "meals for the dead" was held in the triclia.

This was a Roman practice which Christians had adopted. The pagan Romans brought a little food to the burial place of a member of their family. There they ate the food as a sort of religious remembrance of one whom they had loved and lost. Christians took over the practice and celebrated (for a time at least) an agape at such a place.

The triclia at San Sebastiano is a smallish room, with stone benches that go around it. It would have been ideal for the sacred meals, or *refrigeria* (refreshment) . There is no doubt that in the third century, at least, such an observance was held in that place in honor of the two great apostles. One wall scratching says explicitly: "For Peter and Paul, I, of the name of Tomius Caelius, have held a *refrigerium*."

Since it was thought that Peter had been killed nearby, it was natural that such a shrine would have come into being. There is an inscription near the crypt of the basilica of San Sebastiano which goes back to the time of Bishop Damasus. It includes the words: "Whoever you may be who searches for the names of Peter and Paul, you should know that here the holy ones once dwelt." This is generally taken to confirm the notion that the bodies did once rest there. More likely, for a time it was believed, or at least accepted, that the two apostles had been put to rest nearby in the famous Callistus Catacomb in which later Roman bishops had been buried. There is also the possibility that for a time, maybe a few years, the bodies of both were transferred to that place until appropriate arrangements could be made for their disposition elsewhere.

It is unfortunate that very little has yet been done to excavate under the great basilica of Saint Paul Outside the Walls. This is on a very ancient site, supposedly near the place on the road to Ostia where Paul was killed. When the ancient church burned in 1823, some diggings were made but not very systematically. There is now a grand new building, incorporating a good deal of what was left of the old church structure. Excavation might be difficult, but it would be extremely important and useful, especially since there was probably a good deal less plundering and damage done to Saint Paul's than was done to Saint Peter's. During the Middle Ages nobody seemed to regard it as offensive to plunder the old churches in Rome, and Saint Peter's suffered badly.

The excavation work under Saint Peter's basilica began in 1939. Earlier excavations had also been made, some of them as early as 1615 when the present *confessio*—the shrine to Peter in the midst of the great crossing of the basilica—was built. This replaced the old confessio, which was taken down when the new church was constructed. A few years later, in 1626, it was necessary to dig foundations for the bronze pillars that support the famous Bernini canopy of the confessio, under the dome of the church. At that time pagan graves and burial rooms were discovered along with the place identified as the grave of Peter. But it was only in 1939 that work began in a very systematic and scholarly way. Thanks to that effort, which has continued, with interruptions, up to the present time, the topography underneath the basilica is well known.

The present basilica of Saint Peter's has beneath it the remains of the ancient church which the Emperor Constantine built in the fourth century to honor the traditional first bishop of Rome. That church was demolished in 1506 when the present building was begun. It took one hundred and fifty years to complete the work. The Constantinian church was started around the year 333 and completed under Constantius, son of the great emperor. As often has happened when old buildings are replaced, the present Saint Peter's is some three meters above the presumed level of the old building.

In 1939, when it was decided to enlarge the grottoes under the present church, in order to provide space for the burial of Pope Pius XI, very ancient Roman walls were found. The excavations were continued, going beneath the level of the crypt with its grottoes.

There was a thick wall, first thought to be part of a circus which Nero had built, but soon found to be a protecting wall to help in leveling off the slope of the Vatican hill in preparation for the construction of Constantine's church. A slope would have been a perilous base for the structure. The space was filled in with earth. What is interesting is that when the diggers got through the wall and around it, they discovered a cemetery, with two rows of mausoleums which were separated from each other by a narrow passage. The graves were able to be dated; they came from the second and third centuries after Christ.

From inscriptions and other evidence, it was ascertained that many different cults were represented in the mausoleums. There were several Christian graves, too, where Christian believers had probably been interred along with pagan members of their families. There was also a completely Christian mausoleum belonging to the "Julian" family, with Christian mosaics and a probable third-century date.

The excavations continued. A room was found that has been described in the official Vatican statement as a small monument with columns. This means a room, or chamber, supported by pillars with a niche in the front, at the east end of the supporting wall which is painted red. There is a second niche above, like a second story in a dwelling, but on a small scale.

Although all the evidence is not in, some conclusions may be drawn. It would seem that the probabilities are these: 1. Peter was not killed on the Via Appia, but crucified in the vicinity of the Vatican hill, which is by the Neronian palace ruins. 2. Since he had been killed there, he was buried in an already familiar Roman cemetery, which is what, in fact, has been excavated during the work carried on underneath Saint Peter's basilica. 3. The place where he was buried is very likely, if not certainly, the one that has been discovered under the church there. This would make sense, at any rate, and would help to explain why Constantine, in order to honor Peter, constructed the church in just that place, and why it was taken at that time to be the spot where Peter was, in fact, buried. 4. We do not know, nor is there any way in which we could know, whether the bones found there are the bones of Peter himself.

Wherever Peter was buried and whatever conclusions may be accepted concerning his stay in Rome, there is no reason to doubt that he was in that city, that he did have a position of leadership there, and that he did suffer martyrdom in Rome under Nero. And a century or so later, the Christian community in Rome did believe that they were the heirs of this great apostle.

Bibliography

In addition to the book by the Swiss scholar Oscar Cullmann, mentioned in the preface (*Peter: Disciple, Apostle, Martyr*. London: S.C.M. Press; and Philadelphia: Westminster Press, second revised edition, 1962, also available in paperback), there are two readable studies about Peter:

Foakes-Jackson, F. J. *Peter, Prince of Apostles*. New York: Macmillan, 1927.
Lowe, John. *St. Peter*. Oxford: Oxford University Press, 1956.

In the *Interpreter's Bible Dictionary* (Nashville, Tenn.: Abingdon Press, 1962), available in most public libraries, there is an admirable article on the New Testament material about Peter. This should be consulted for the most up-to-date and adequate discussion of what is historically known about our subject, apart from legendary stories and archaeological evidence.

A charmingly written discussion of Saint Peter and the Roman Church, with a description of the archaeological material in Rome, is Walter Lowrie's *SS. Peter and Paul in Rome*. New York: Oxford University Press, 1940. Since the publication of this book, new material has come to light, some of which is mentioned in Cullmann's work but much of which is so recent that no popular book is yet available on the discoveries excepting in Italian. It is to be hoped that before long there will be a popular, yet scholarly, English volume that will summarize the story of the excavations made in the last few years under Saint Peter's basilica in Rome. At the time of writing the present book, the most that can be said is that there is every reason to believe that the burial place of Saint Peter has been discovered and that Pope Paul VI had every reason to say, with assurance, that this is indeed the original Petrine shrine. This is said despite some of the conclusions reached by D. W. O'Connor in his enormous, very learned, and expansive book, *Peter in Rome: The Literary, Liturgical, and Archaeological Evidence*. New York: Columbia University Press, 1969, whose findings are that Simon Peter lived and ministered in Rome, was very likely *not* a bishop there, *probably* was martyred and buried there, but that the shrine at Saint Peter's is *improbably* his burial place. It is with the second and the final conclusions that the present writer would differ. Why should not the ancient tradition be trusted here?

Index